GOD USES DEPRESSION

by Andrew Kowach

One Christian's testimony of how God used his time in the clutches of clinical depression to set him spiritually, emotionally and mentally free.

This book is dedicated to all those
who are desperate to find freedom from their
mental and emotional struggles.

Table of Contents

Introduction

The only friends I had during the darkest days of my life were a family of squirrels that lived in a tree outside my living room window. I watched them endure all types of weather, including the bitter northeastern winters. Strong winds often accompanied the snowstorms and their nest would come dangerously close to being ripped apart. I imagined them huddled together inside hoping their home wouldn't be destroyed. Even though I watched them from the warmth and safety of my apartment, my depression made me feel like I was out in the relentless freezing weather as well. My depression was one long brutal winter and I was fully exposed to all of its harsh elements but without any shelter or anyone to curl up with.

I hadn't always been in that place of unyielding depression though; its symptoms started when I was young. In elementary school when I saw other kids on the playground laughing and having fun I didn't feel as joyful and carefree as they looked. I tried to act happy to fit in but was never quite able to and I didn't know why. I did have breaks in my sadness though and was able to have some fun, but that was the exception. Other kids often didn't look at things the way I did; I just thought it was because I was blessed with a heightened understanding of life. I felt if others saw things the way I did we would get along. The fact was that others didn't think the way I did because my depression negatively distorted my thoughts and actions.

If I wrote down all the experiences I had that my depression had a negative impact on this book would have been extremely long and redundant in nature. I have spent years identifying and narrowing down my thoughts and depression-related experiences so I can present in the clearest and most precise manner how my depression progressed. To be able to bring forth the most accurate details though, I had to put myself back into this dark and torturous time of my life. I didn't use an editor or ghost-writer either because they would detract from my story and tone of authenticity. If God hadn't continually prompted me to write this book I would have tried to forget what I went through. If I didn't relive this part of my life though I wouldn't have been able to share my story with those whose lives have been touched by depression in some way. Because of my personal experience in the dark my heart goes out deeply to the millions of people who are battling this terrible affliction. No matter how much I empathize and sympathize with all those suffering from it though; God's heart goes out immeasurably more.

Growing up

I grew up in a middle-class neighborhood in upstate New York and was the youngest of four in my family. When I was young my entire world consisted of my school, neighborhood and best friends who lived next-door. Whenever my friends and I weren't in school we spent most of our time playing in my big backyard and in the nearby woods. Our thoughts never wandered much beyond what we wanted to play that day. As we got older though we played less and spent more time exploring the world outside my backyard.

My mother remarried when I was twelve and we moved to my stepfather's house. He lived about twenty minutes away which put me in a new school district. When I was in elementary school I had a difficult time making friends and I was afraid it would be even worse at my new school and I was right. No matter how much I reached out to make friends though no one really wanted to do more than make small talk in class and in the halls. I tried to act 'cool' so kids would want to hang-out with me but it didn't work; I just circled around the outside of different social groups and couldn't find a way into any of them.

After about a year I thought I finally found someone who genuinely wanted to be my friend. His name was John and one day after school he invited me over to his house. When we got there we ate some snacks and watched television. After a while he invited to go outside because he wanted to show me something. We went out to his backyard and he took out something from his pocket that looked like a small tobacco pipe. I asked him what it was and he told me it was a pot pipe. He had a small bag of marijuana and proceeded to pack some into the pipe. He lit it and took a big puff then handed it to me; I resisted at first but gave into the pressure. I really enjoyed how the pot made me feel so I began to go to his house every day after school to smoke with him.

John had big parties on the weekends and I met many of the popular kids there that I had never talked with in school before. I felt a lot of students now thought I was cool because I was a regular fixture at his parties. I hadn't expected drinking beer and smoking pot would be a central part of my new friendship with John but it didn't matter because I thought I finally found a true friend and somewhere I fit in.

Before I started partying I was easily the best runner on the track team. After only about a month of smoking almost every day my breathing became labored and I regularly finished races in second and third place. My academics were slipping as well because I had a difficult time concentrating in class. I began feeling especially down after each high wore off and over time it was taking me longer to feel normal again. One time I felt especially low and for the first time I realized it was a side-effect of smoking pot. I started smoking because it made me feel better but now the low wasn't worth the high, so I quit.

After I had stopped partying with my 'friends' they didn't want to be around me. When I saw them in the hallways they walked by without saying hello. They no longer considered me part of their group because I didn't smoke and drink with them anymore. I missed feeling like I fit in and I was very tempted to start smoking again but I didn't because I knew what it would do to me. I went back to spending most of my time alone.

I started skipping school every Monday because I didn't want to face another week of having to put on a happy face. One of the Mondays I stayed home I was exceedingly depressed and discouraged. I couldn't bear not fitting in any longer and always fighting off my sadness. I thought the only way to escape my pain was to kill myself. After considering different ways, I chose to overdose on pills because I thought it would be the least painful. I got a bottle of aspirin and made seven piles of ten on the kitchen counter. I stared down at them while trying to gather the courage to follow through with it. To overcome my fear I tried to detach myself from what I was about to do. I proceeded to pick up the first pile, threw them in my mouth and forced them down with some water.

After swallowing all the pills I went to my

bedroom to lay on my bed and wait to die. As I anticipated the inevitable, my cat Peter jumped up on the bed and snuggled up next to me like he knew something was very wrong. Suddenly, out of nowhere, I heard a stern and commanding voice say "Get up, you're not giving up this easy!" (Looking back I know it was God speaking to me) The words rocked me to my soul and my heart was gripped with the intense reality I might soon die. I responded to the direct order and immediately jumped out of bed and ran to the bathroom to try and make myself throw-up.

When I reached the bathroom I tried to force myself to vomit, but couldn't relax enough to do so. After a few frantic and unsuccessful attempts I started to panic far beyond what I ever had. I knew the only chance for survival now was to call 911. After I called I anxiously waited for the ambulance to arrive. Each second seemed like an hour because all the pills in me felt like a ticking time-bomb. When the paramedics arrived I quickly explained to them what I had done; they then gave me a medication that induces vomiting. They made me drink five glasses of water and put me in the ambulance. I was given a pail to hold between my legs to vomit in and by the time we arrived at the hospital my stomach was completely empty. After the doctor examined me he said I was no longer in any physical danger, but wanted to keep me overnight for observation. Some people came to visit me when I was there and that made me feel special because I wasn't used to such expressions of care and concern. After I was released I returned to the life I had just tried to escape.

Even though I was back in the same situation I now knew killing myself was not the answer to taking away my pain. I still felt the same as before, so I had to continue my battle of trying different ways to feel better. Despite my perpetual sadness, I still didn't have a problem meeting girls. I was good looking, in good shape and able to put on a happy face when I wanted or needed to. When I did have a girlfriend, we spent most of our time alone, in and out of school. My girlfriends usually made me feel better and took my mind off my problems for a while, but my sadness always returned. Even when I had their company, I still often felt alone.

When I was in high school I met someone who seemed like he genuinely wanted to be my friend. One day he invited me to go over to his house after school to ride his dirt bike. We had a fun time riding his dirt bike that initial visit, so I went over a couple times a week after that. We were playing pool in his cellar one day after school and he said to me, "You're really cool some days and others you're not, why can't you be like that all the time?" I analyzed my behavior and tried to duplicate how I acted the days I believed he thought I was cool. No matter what I tried though he stopped wanting to be around me. An unfortunate symptom of my depression was that I had low self-esteem, so when he said that I took it to heart and it deeply saddened me. No matter who I was around deep down I often felt that whatever they said and did was right and how I thought and acted was wrong.

I continued to be miserable all the way through high school and couldn't wait for it to be over. I had enough credits to graduate mid-senior year and I saw it as an opportunity to get away as soon as possible. I applied to the State University of New York at Plattsburg and was accepted to start that January. The thought of going away to college sustained me the last few months of high school. I believed I would be escaping everything and everyone that was holding me back from being happy.

College years

The day finally arrived when it was time to leave for college. I was thrilled I was about to start my new life, but nervous at the same time because I didn't know what to expect. I didn't have my license yet, so my sister Caroline drove me. She started college the previous year so I took advantage of our two-hour trip to ask about her college experiences. She helped calm my nerves by telling me some of what I should expect, but my stomach still increasingly tightened the closer we got. When we arrived, I located my dormitory on the campus map and we went straight over. When we pulled into the parking lot I was surprised to see that my dormitory was ten stories high. The college was in a scenic part of upstate New York; so I could enjoy the surrounding splendor because my assigned room was on the tenth floor.

When we unpacked the car it took a few trips on the elevator to move all my things in. Once we were finished my sister had to get started back; so after we said our goodbyes I watched her drive away until she was out of sight. As I stood in the parking lot, I was overcome with loneliness because I was in a completely foreign world with no one I knew.

When I went back up to my room the first thing I did was crack open my journal for the first time since I got it. Someone had given it to me in high school and since everything was so mundane at that time, I had nothing to write. Now that I was starting my new life in college I felt it was the perfect time to begin.

1/20/88

Hey Nate, (I had named my journal "Nate") How's it going? Guess what, I'm in college now!

My depression didn't go away when I went to college; It just got pushed under the surface by the excitement of my new life. Instead of my studies being my priority that first semester, I focused more on going to the bars at least a couple times a week to get drunk, have fun and hopefully meet some women. To get into the bars I changed my date of birth on my license and for a few extra bucks, others as well. Most of us freshmen didn't drink much before college, but we did then and often. We did many foolish things when we were drunk and something I did was take women I'd met at the bars back to my room for the night. My conscience and better judgment were difficult to find that first semester.

The novelty of college life wore off by my second semester. I was no longer distracted by partying and one-night stands, so my depression reemerged. To try and fight it off I did what I frequently did during high school to try and make myself feel better, get a girlfriend. When I had dated in the past, I subconsciously made the relationship progress rapidly because I wanted to feel that happiness and contentment that often comes from the closeness that develops between couples over a period of time. The problem with that thinking was; I wasn't capable of experiencing that type of happiness because my depression took away my ability to. My girlfriends usually gave me a lot of love and affection but unfortunately for them I couldn't reciprocate it. My depression kept me from seeing all the facets of my relationships clearly; which was a barrier to understanding the type of care and attention they deserved and needed. Because of my negative and warped view of life, I was frequently in a bad mood which caused a lot of arguments. I am sure my girlfriends were often insecure around me because it was impossible to predict how I would act at any given moment.

By the end of my second year I still hadn't declared a major so I had to make my decision soon or I wouldn't have enough time to complete a major. I did very well in my art classes in high school and college so I thought maybe a major in art would be a good idea. Even though I enjoyed art and was good at it, I also liked working with people. I wondered how I could combine these interests and talents and I thought being an art teacher would be a good fit. Plattsburg didn't have an Art Education program so I had to find a school that did. I researched different schools and discovered the State University of New York at New Paltz had one. Since my depression had returned I thought a fresh start at a new college might help me feel better.

3/9/91

Do I need to be consoled through my journal entries or is it a need for self-expression? I wonder, why oh why is all this happening to me? This constant torment is like someone always pushing, pushing—never letting me rest, never, never. I am pursuing I don't know what, do you? Oh please tell me. Good, bad, up, down—what are we searching for? Why so many questions and no answers?

Once I was at New Paltz I got good grades and got along well with the other students in the Art Education program. From the outside it appeared I had finally found a place where I fit in and my education was on track. Even though I now had all the components of a good college experience, my depression remained. I had a full class schedule and was always around other students but as always, still felt alone. As well as depression I also began struggling with anxiety. The first time I had a bout with it was when one night I couldn't get to sleep because I was overcome with worry about being able to balance my job with my studies. Exercise always helped me relax so I put on my shoes and went out into the cool night for a jog. I went to the track next to my dormitory and the moon shown so bright that the white lines that delineated the lanes were as clear as they were during the day. I pushed myself hard as I ran and was surprised at how long it took to relax. After about a half-hour I finally felt calm enough to go back to sleep.

I had lived in the dorms since the beginning of college and I got very tired of it; so I decided to move off campus. I didn't have enough money to get an apartment on my own though, so I searched for someone who wanted to move off as well. I met with a few acquaintances who already had an apartment and were looking for another roommate. After we talked I thought it would be a good fit, so I decided to move in with them. Even though we didn't know one another well, it didn't concern me much because I was excited to just be getting out of the dorms. The apartment was in a rural area about five miles from campus, but I didn't think much of any impact it might have on my college experience.

Campus was in the middle of a small town and I could walk to all my classes or anywhere else I wanted to. Since I now lived far from school, I could no longer do anything without having to drive there. My new roommates were all friends and weren't interested in getting to know me, they just wanted my rent contribution. I soon realized moving there was a big mistake. Being far from school and spending much of my time alone amplified my depression. The following fall semester I didn't make the same mistake though, I moved into an apartment across the street from campus.

I was done with my classroom studies in the spring 1992 and all I had left to complete was my student teaching in the fall. My brother lived in California and he invited me to come out and stay with him for that summer. He lived in the small coastal town of Moss Beach, located just north of San Francisco. His apartment was only a few blocks from the beach and I could smell the fresh ocean air each night as I drifted off to sleep. My cousins lived nearby as well and I hadn't seen them since I went on a vacation there when I was six. My mother had a photo of all of us from when we were there. In the picture we were all piled up on top of each on the beach. Almost every day when I wasn't working I went down to the beach. I walked barefoot in the sand and enjoyed the warm sun and sights and sounds of the ocean. I was alone much of the time but the beauty of the area was a pleasant distraction. Following is a journal entry of when I lived there.

7/28/92

If only, all souls could get along with one another... No more spirits sitting alone and wondering, "Is there anyone else out there who is like me?" Good night for now...

After my warm and sunny summer in California I went back to New York to complete my last semester of college. The previous spring all the students in the Art Education program were assigned a school district where they would complete their student teaching. My district was in the small town of Grahamsville, located in the Catskill Mountains in southern New York. I didn't like staying where there wasn't a lot of people, so the thought of living in the mountains was not appealing. When I drove down at the beginning of the semester the deeper I traveled into the mountains, the further away my time in the warmth and sun in California seemed.

When I arrived in Grahamsville I drove down the main street and stopped at the single blinking red light in the middle of town. All I saw was a general store, a few different shops, a fire station and a small post office. After my brief scan I continued on to the house where my college had found for me to live that semester. This living arrangement felt odd because I never met this man I would be staying with. Once I arrived at his house I walked up the stone path leading to the front door and knocked. A gentleman answered and politely invited me in. After introductions and talking a short while he showed me to my room. It used to be his daughter's and it appeared nothing had been moved since she left. Due to the decor and age of her belongings, it appeared she had moved out about fifteen years prior. There was everything from her dolls to trophies she had won in high school. It felt strange that first night as I lie in that bed because I was in a room frozen in time and the old dolls on the dresser seemed like they were looking back at me. I felt so alone because I was in this stranger's house deep within the mountains.

My first six weeks I taught in the elementary school. My cooperating teacher, Kathy, was very kind and supportive and she brightened up my small and lonely world. During school one day I confided in her I was very uncomfortable where I was staying and that I wanted to move out. I asked her if she knew of anywhere I could stay for the remainder of the semester, but she said no. The following day in school she invited me over for dinner to meet her family and I gladly accepted. I was thrilled because I didn't know anyone else. After school that day I went back to where I was staying and watched the clock in great anticipation of that evening. The moment it was time to leave, I went right over.

When I was at Kathy's house she introduced me to her husband Paul and his daughter. We all then went into the dining room to eat dinner. I was so excited because I hadn't had a good home-cooked meal in a long time. All I ate since I arrived in town was canned food and spaghetti. Over dinner I enjoyed getting to know her family because Kathy talked about them frequently in school. Knowing all of them made my teaching experience much more enjoyable.

The following day in school I thanked Kathy for the wonderful meal and visit and she said her family really enjoyed it as well. She then unexpectedly asked if I wanted to stay with her family for the remainder of the semester! Out of the kindness of their hearts they opened their home to me during my time of need. I was so shocked and excited at the offer and I accepted without hesitation. The following day after school I went back to where I was staying, quickly packed my things and went right over. Right away they made me feel comfortable and at home.

They included me in all the household activities, even the chores. I know people usually don't like housework, but helping out made me feel like part of the family and not just a guest. One day we had to rake leaves in the backyard and I would have usually cringed at the thought because growing up I spent many autumn hours raking in my backyard. I didn't mind this time though because they had shown me so much love and hospitality that it was the least I could do. As I raked I pushed down so hard on my rake that it broke, so they gave me another and I broke that one as well. I thought they were going to be really upset with me when I broke the second, but instead they had a hearty laugh and were very gracious about it. I finished the job without breaking the third!

My time there refreshed my spirit and gave me respite from my depression and anxiety. My lasting impression of living with them is a feeling of being unconditionally loved, accepted and supported. I'll always be grateful to them for all the love they showed me and the impact they had on my life.

After I had finished my six weeks of student teaching in the elementary school and six in the high school, I had completed my last requirement for college. I stayed late on my last day in high school so I could gather my things. As I started down the hallway it was very quiet because most of the people had already left for the day. All I heard was my footsteps and a couple voices echoing from the end of the hall. I stopped in front of a display case that contained some artwork from an assignment I'd given my students. I had a sense of pride because they created these imaginative pieces using the skills I taught them.

After reflecting on some of the memories from when I was there, I unceremoniously walked out the large front doors and down the long set of steps. When I reached my car I leaned up against it and let the sun warm my face as I soaked in the reality that I just finished college. After I thought about what I had just accomplished, my focus turned to what I was going to do next in life.

Truth revealed

When I lived with my brother in California I had met a woman where I worked and we started dating. When I went back to do my student teaching we kept our relationship alive by talking almost daily on the phone. We got along so well on the phone that we discussed me moving in with her when I graduated. The idea of going out to California was very appealing because I believed it would solve the two major issues I was facing; what to do with my life and how to find my elusive happiness. When I graduated we took a leap of faith and decided I would move in with her.

Once I moved out to California my girlfriend and I got along well for the first few months, but our relationship began to soon unravel. We didn't get to know one another nearly as well as we should have so our relationship was set up to fail. After we broke up I rented a room. One day as I sat alone in the small space I called home I asked myself "why am I still in California?" I didn't have a good job, girlfriend or any other good reason to stay, so I decided to move back to New York. I didn't want to move back close to my hometown though because I would have felt like I failed in my pursuit of happiness.

My sister's fiancé lived in Rochester, New York and he let me stay with him. Rochester is located about two hours west from where I grew up so I still felt my quest wasn't a failure. I stayed with him for about three months and then decided the area wasn't right for me. I thought a good place to try next was Buffalo New York, because my brother lived there. Once in Buffalo I got an apartment, full-time job and even a girlfriend. I lived there about six months but still couldn't escape my darkness. In a last ditch effort to be free of my depression, I decided to move back to where I grew up in an attempt to capture some of the happiness I experienced there as a child.

I moved to Schenectady New York; a small city located next to my hometown Niskayuna. Since I barely had enough money for gas to get there, the only place I could stay was with a friend from high school. My friend, Sara, had female roommates and they were uncomfortable at the idea of me living on their couch, so Sara said the only option for me was to stay on her back porch. The porch was enclosed so it wasn't like she was kicking me out into the rain. It wasn't the ideal living situation, but I was thankful to have somewhere to stay. Sara was very kind and spending time with her helped me get my mind off my problems.

I didn't want to live on her porch forever though; so I immediately began searching for a job and found one within a few days. I didn't make much at my new job, so the only place I found in my price range was a studio apartment in the poorer part of the city. Besides the location, the reason why the rent was cheap was because the studio was so small and in poor condition. I had to paint it and do some substantial cleaning before I could move in. I had lived in so many places prior to then, that I wanted to make it comfortable enough that I felt I could settle in there for a while. I lived in three houses before college; eight dorm rooms, two apartments and two houses during college and five different apartments after college.

8/4/94
(A journal entry from when I lived in Schenectady.)

"I feel like a naive newborn and I am vulnerable on every side. Why can't we all love openly and unconditionally and be one? I want everyone's spirits to be free. I have so much love to give. I must learn to take care of myself more and be happy, let my love and spirit soar and break free from the daily obstacles. I don't like anger. I don't like mean people, I hurt from it. This is the first time I have been real honest about the world.

Why do I feel like a pile of dust on someone's hand and they could blow me away anytime they choose? I still have this sick feeling inside, but I think it is from the hurt and pain I experienced growing up. I can remember when I was young I would wake

up in the mornings and be happy and full of energy..... Then something would always happen and upset me and then begin to feel sad again. I can count the times on one hand I really have felt free-spirited and genuinely happy. I am scared of the world out there and the people in it. I cannot take being hurt anymore, it is too painful. I am not superman; I can and do get hurt so much. I have to go to bed. God give me the strength to make it through the next day and please help the pain go away"
– Andrew

Up until I moved into my studio I had tried for years to find happiness in different ways such as girlfriends, partying, exercising, sports, eating the right foods, finding the right job, meeting new people, living in different areas, self-help books, philosophy and any other way I could think of. In the back of my mind I was continually in deep introspection, trying to figure out the exact way to make myself happy. Many of the things I tried worked temporarily but didn't give me the lasting happiness and peace I desired. With each attempt at trying to feel happier, I felt like I was shooting at a moving target that I could never hit.

My search made me feel like I was running a marathon alone and I didn't know where the finish line was. Tirelessly I ran night and day in the rain, snow, heat and in all conditions. I saw and experienced many things along the way but never could fully enjoy them because of my never-ending sadness and restlessness. I had been on my inner quest for happiness for so long that I was running out of the energy and will to go any further. One place I hadn't looked yet was in church, so I decided to give it a try. I wasn't going because I was searching for God, but I thought deeper issues of the heart and soul were addressed there. I hadn't gone regularly since I was a young boy and what I remember most was that I always couldn't wait until the end of service. When I was older the only time I might have attended was on Christmas and/or Easter. I believed going to church was something people did only for conscious or ritual sake and not because it had any practical relevance in modern-day life. I believed in God and tried to respect him, but I felt his life and mine didn't intersect.

I lived near the church I went to when I was young, so I attended service there the following Sunday. During the sermon the preacher told a nice story but it didn't touch my heart and soul as I hoped. I started getting that old familiar bored feeling and couldn't wait for the service to end. I would have walked out during the sermon but that would have been disrespectful. When it was over I headed straight for the door, trying to avoid eye contact so no one would try and strike up a conversation. The pastor was shaking everyone's hands as they exited so I snuck out along the other side of the entrance, out of hands-reach. As I walked down the alley back to my apartment I was especially depressed and disheartened because I felt I might never find happiness.

9/8/94
(Entry when I got back from church)

"I feel depressed beyond belief; It feels like I am just barely holding the threads of sanity together"
- Me

That night I sat on my bed overcome by despair and hopelessness. I was desperate to talk with someone to help me feel better and the only people who came to mind were Paul and Kathy. It had been three years since I graduated college and I had called them a few times when I was hurting. I could always count on their compassion and attentiveness no matter what I was going through. I had no idea what they could say this time to help but I was going to reach out anyway. When I called I was greatly relieved when Paul answered. I explained my desperate state and that I was petrified I would never escape my unrelenting sadness. Paul said if I needed to, I could come down that night. Even though it was nine o'clock and they lived over two hours away, I still accepted the invitation because I was desperate to feel better. I rushed around my apartment grabbing a few essentials and hurried down the three flights of stairs and out to my car. I was overcome by anxiety and fear so I had to fight to keep control of my emotions so I wouldn't crash. It was dark on the mountain roads and they were treacherously curvy, but I ignored all the hazards as I sped along. After what seemed like much longer than it was, I finally arrived at their house.

Paul answered the door and invited me in where Kathy was waiting as well. After a couple hugs I started pouring out my heart about how awful and hopeless I felt. We went to the other room to continue our conversation and as we entered I slumped down onto the floor because I was emotionally and mentally exhausted. I told them I had been searching for happiness for years but never found it no matter what I did, where I went or whom I talked with. Paul said he understood what I was talking about and he knew the answer. He asked me what I knew about the Bible and I told him I only knew major things like Noah and the Ark, Joseph and Mary, baby Jesus, God performing miracles and Jesus dying on the cross. Paul said there was much more than that and the answer to what I was searching for was in there as well. When I lived with them during my student teaching in college they went to church every Sunday but I didn't go with them. I knew they were Christians but I was quick to change the subject when they tried to talk to me about God. This time, when Paul told me the answer to peace and happiness was in the Bible, I was very attentive because I felt this was my last chance to find the peace and happiness I had been searching for.

He began explaining how in the beginning God created all things, including man and woman. He named man Adam and women Eve and placed them in the Garden of Eden. God told them they could eat from any of the trees in the garden except from the tree of the knowledge of good and evil. Even though God commanded them not to eat from that one tree, Eve did and then convinced Adam to as well. By disobeying God's direct command, they committed the first sins in this world. Since God cannot live in the presence of sin He drove them from the garden. Once their personal relationship with God was broken, there became a void in their heart where it once was. He explained there is still a God-shaped void in the hearts of those who haven't asked God to forgive them.

"So He drove the man out; and at the east of the garden of Eden He stationed the cherubim and the flaming sword which turned every direction to guard the way to the tree of life."
- Genesis 3:24

Paul continued to explain that when God forced them out, their relationship with him was broken. Paul explained that God's plan to restore that relationship was to send his only son Jesus, to die on the cross to pay the penalty for the sins of the world. Even though the Bible says Jesus died for the sins of the world he told me each individual still has to believe in their own heart that He did. He showed me the following verses that supported what he said:

"because, if you confess with your mouth that Jesus is Lord and believe in your heart that God raised him from the dead, you will be saved."
- Romans 10:9

"This is good and it is pleasing in the sight of God our Savior, who desires all people to be saved and to come to the knowledge of the truth." - 1 Timothy 2:3-4

I didn't understand everything he was explaining but I desperately needed peace and happiness so I told him I wanted God's forgiveness. Kathy was sitting behind me on the couch and she put her hands on my shoulders and Paul was sitting next to me on the floor. Having them so close made me feel tucked in by their love. Paul said he was going to pray the following prayer and if I wanted to, follow along with him.

"Dear God, I know I am a sinner and I believe Jesus died on the cross to pay for my sins. Please come into my heart and save my soul."

As soon as I asked God to come into my heart, I felt a warm sensation start at my feet and wash up over me all the way to the top of my head. Until that moment I didn't remember ever crying in my life, so it surprised me when I felt a single tear roll down my cheek. I became so relaxed that I sat on the floor motionless, soaking in the total peace I felt immersed in. When I gathered my thoughts I searched for the words to describe what I just experienced, but I struggled to. Paul told me the Holy Spirit had just come into my heart. He said that not everyone experiences the sensation I did but the Holy Spirit does come and dwell in anyone who asks God to forgive them. I felt a deep joy and peace in my soul like I never had. I believed that my long journey to find happiness was over. We talked late into the night about what occurred until it was time to go to bed. As I lie waiting to drift off, I hoped with all that I was that the joy and deep contentment in my soul I now felt would still be there in the morning.

"Peace I leave with you; my peace I give to you. Not as the world gives do I give to you. Let not your hearts be troubled, neither let them be afraid." - John 14:27

"and you will know the truth and the truth will set you free." - John 8:32

When I awoke the next morning I immediately took an inner assessment to see if the joy and peace I'd experienced the night before remained and it did! I quickly went downstairs to the dining room where Paul and Kathy were eating breakfast. They said "Good morning" with big smiles on because of the wonderful event that occurred the night before. I had so many questions but didn't know where to begin. I felt like it was my first day of spiritual kindergarten and I had everything to learn. During the entire breakfast I listened closely as they explained what happened to me spiritually. I asked if I would always feel this good and they said all my problems weren't just going to vanish, but the Holy Spirit would always be with me and help me through them. They said my life was going to be different from then on and I would experience it like I never had. They said I needed to pray and read my Bible daily so I could grow in faith and learn more about my Heavenly Father. They explained that I also had to find a Bible-based church so I could receive support from other believers and grow as a Christian. After they taught me much about what I was experiencing and answered as many of my questions as they could, we finished our breakfast and I got ready to leave. I thanked them for all their love, support and especially for introducing me to my Savior. As I drove home along the mountain road I savored the deep joy and peace that now filled my heart and soul.

When I arrived back at my apartment I started doing what Paul and Kathy told me I needed to do to start growing as a Christian. I tried to pray but I never had before so I attempted to imitate how I saw people on television and in church do it. Even though I felt I didn't know how, I kept trying because I wanted to thank God for what he had done for me. I also started reading the Bible they gave me; I had attempted to in the past, but I couldn't understand it. This time when I read the Bible I was amazed because I could understand it! They had only been words on a page to me before but now they opened up a whole new world. I could understand things that were more wonderful than anything I could have ever imagined. The mysteries to life were being revealed to me with each turn of the page. Where there had always been questions, there was now answers. I used to wish there was a guidebook to life and now it was in my hands! I had only viewed life through my eyes, but now God was allowing me to see it through his!

"And we know that the Son of God has come and has given us understanding, so that we may know him who is true; and we are in him who is true, in his Son Jesus Christ. He is the true God and eternal life." - 1 John 5:20

When I started reading the Bible I quickly learned how much God hates sin. The first and most obvious one I knew I was committing was that I cursed, a lot. Now when I swore I felt the Holy Spirit in me convicting my heart of the sin. I didn't just try to stop my sinful behaviors because God didn't want me to, but I hated the feeling of conviction. When I tried to change my sinful behaviors though I still felt pulled between wanting to act the way I used to, with the way I now knew God wanted me to.

I'm sure people that knew me before I was a Christian observed the new way I talked about God and how I behaved differently and thought I was being brainwashed and blindly following a religion like a robot. If being brainwashed by what the Bible says means having peace and joy in my heart and a hope for the future, then I was exceedingly thankful to be! My personality didn't change but God started transforming my heart, thoughts and character into more like his. Because of the many changes I felt occurring in me, I now understood why the Bible says that once someone's sins are forgiven they are 'born again'.

"Nicodemus said to Him, "How can a man be born when he is old? He cannot enter a second time into his mother's womb and be born, can he?" Jesus answered, "Truly, truly, I say to you, unless one is born of water and the Spirit he cannot enter into the kingdom of God. "That which is born of the flesh is flesh and that which is born of the Spirit is spirit."
- John 3:4-6

I was so excited about what God had done for me that I figured everyone would want to experience the same joy and freedom I now had. I went over to my neighbors' to tell him what the Lord had done for me but the more I shared, the more uncomfortable he looked. He listened politely for a while and then changed the subject. I couldn't believe he didn't respond with the elation and enthusiasm I thought he would. I was disappointed with his lack of response but I was determined to tell others about what the Lord had done for me. I told my good news to a few more people but I was perplexed because they weren't receptive as well. I was frustrated because no one really wanted to hear about how much joy the Lord had given me and how he could do the same for them as well. I began to feel spiritually alone and then I understood why Paul and Kathy told me I needed to find a Bible-based church.

I searched the phone book for a church and came across one that looked promising, so I attended the following Sunday. When the pastor began to preach I was amazed because I never heard anything like it. I was astonished because it was touching my heart and soul as I had always desired a teaching would. After the service I approached the pastor and introduced myself and told him I had recently received God's forgiveness. I told him I was having a difficult time adjusting to my new spiritual life though. He reassured me that what I was going through was a normal part of a new life in Christ. I was relieved and comforted after I talked with him because I began to worry if anyone else felt or could relate to what I was going through. I thanked God because I no longer felt spiritually alone.

Reality check

After attending church for about a month cracks developed in my shiny perception of what I thought it would be like. I saw people caught up in worrying more about acting like 'a good Christian' rather than focusing on the Lord. When we sang worship songs I would discreetly look around to see who was singing and who wasn't; I was surprised to see how many weren't and most of the ones who were, looked like their hearts weren't in it. I couldn't understand why everyone wasn't enthusiastically expressing anything but sheer joy and gratitude for Jesus dying on the cross for them. I was disheartened and baffled by what I saw, but I didn't let it stop me from praising God with my whole heart.

"Praise the LORD! I will give thanks to the LORD with my whole heart, in the company of the upright, in the congregation." - Psalm 111:1

When I first started going to church everyone was very nice and accepting, but I soon learned that everyone wasn't as friendly as they appeared. After service one day I was invited to a fellowship; I thought it would be a great opportunity to get to know some other Christians. We all met the following Saturday night in a classroom in the church school. We had something to eat and drink and I talked with some people I hadn't met before. After visiting a while the group leader announced we were going to gather in a group and talk about how God is working in each of our lives. We arranged the chairs in a circle and then started going around and sharing. The closer it was to my turn the more nervous I became; but excited as well because I thought I was going to receive the help I needed from my new spiritual family. I was hopeful I would find biblical answers and solutions to my problems because most of the people in the group had been Christians for a substantial amount of time and they could use their broad understanding of Scripture to help me resolve some issues that had plagued me most of my life.

When it was my turn to speak I first told everyone how wonderful my experience was when I asked God to forgave me of my sins; I should have stopped there. I explained that even though I felt an indescribable peace and joy when the Holy Spirit came to live in me, I began to feel sad and anxious again. I told them I felt trapped in a dark place and I didn't know how to escape. As I continued to share details about what I was going through everyone's faces went blank and I could tell they didn't know how to process what I was saying. When they tried to respond I saw how uncomfortable they were and they stammered as they tried to give feedback and advice. I knew right then how wrong I was to believe I would receive the answers and guidance I needed from the group. I became so uncomfortable that I wished there was a back door I could have slipped out of, but unfortunately there wasn't.

The next day in church I heard what I'd shared with the group traveling through the rumor mill. I noticed others who weren't even there looking at me judgmentally. I was very saddened by the widening gulf between how I was being treated and what I read in the Bible about how Christians should treat one another. Since I hadn't found the support I needed from my peers I thought that maybe an older Christian might have the answers I needed. I had previously talked with a gentleman in the church who was about sixty-five and he had been attending the church for about twenty years. I thought because he was a much older and seasoned believer that he would be a much better person to talk to about my problems. Even though I barely knew him, I approached him anyways and told him I needed a Christian's perspective about a few things I was struggling with and if I could talk to him about them. He said I could and invited me over for lunch after service.

I went to his house and during lunch began sharing what was on my heart. I told him about my poor experience with my peers at church that one Saturday night and how I didn't find the answers I was searching for. I poured out my heart as much as possible to give him the clearest picture of what I was going through so he could give me the most precise insight into my issues. One of the problems I shared was that my continual mental and emotion suffering was so draining that it made it difficult for me to hold a full-time job.

After I revealed much of my deep and personal struggles he spoke up for the first time. Without compassion and even with a slight tone of indignation he made the pronouncement "Well, if you worked a full-time job you wouldn't be having all these problems!" I was completely taken aback by what he said. At that moment he revealed his total lack of sensitivity and understanding. I had shared my heart with this man and he totally disregarded it. Once I got over my initial shock, I realized how wrong I was to assume that just because he was an older Christian and had been going to the church a long time, that he would have the godly wisdom and compassion I needed. After he spoke those hurtful words I politely thanked him for the lunch and left. I felt crushed as I drove away and worse than I did before I went over. I was extremely disappointed and saddened that I once again, didn't receive the help I needed from my fellow Christians.

Since I didn't know where else to turn for support and answers I resorted back to trying to find comfort in a woman. I didn't just want to date this time though, I wanted to get married because I felt it was the key to happiness. I figured the best place to find a Christian wife was in church, so I now had two goals when I went, worship the Lord and look for a wife. There weren't many women in my age range there but I was so desperate to find my future bride that I zeroed in on one that I convinced myself I was attracted to. Her name was Lesley and after just a couple weeks of getting to know each other we started dating.

We pushed our relationship along rapidly and bypassed most of the important elements that make a solid foundation of a healthy relationship. After the first month of dating we started arguing frequently but we still stayed together. Before we met we were both eager to find a spouse so despite our fighting, we began discussing marriage. We believed that if we got married God would miraculously make our relationship work.

One night when I was contemplating proposing I took a long walk to pray and ask God if it was his will that I marry Lesley. I listened intently for His response and I thought I heard his small voice in my heart say "Yes, go ahead." (In retrospect I know the reply I thought was from God, was only my own desire to be married screaming over sound wisdom). I think if I saw the words 'Don't do it' painted in huge red letters I still wouldn't have gotten the message. I was so desperate to be free from my ever-present darkness though that I think at that point nothing could have stopped me.

Even though every warning sign was flashing not to get married, I proceeded to purchase an engagement ring. I chose the place to propose and took Lesley there under the guise we were just going for a nice picnic. When we arrived I led her up a path to a large rock outcrop over a mountain lake. As we enjoyed the beauty I got down on one knee and took her left hand. I ignored every molecule in my being screaming not to do it and in a shaky voice proceeded to ask her to marry me and she exclaimed she would. We then proceeded to take a leap of faith into the deep waters of a hazardous and uncertain marriage.

After our wedding we went to Hawaii for our honeymoon. On the first morning I arose early and went out onto the balcony to enjoy the view. As the sun warmed my body I listened to the calm early morning waves gently lapping against the ocean shore. The scenery was so beautiful that I felt I had been transported into a different world. I saw a wide array of trees, tropical plants and a beautiful island landscape. There was a silhouette of an ancient volcano that had been overgrown by years of vegetation growth. I was surrounded by such beauty that even my problems couldn't have stopped me from relishing the splendor. After my short out-of-body escape, my thoughts turned back to my marriage and realization that it wasn't the key to happiness.

One evening we went to a luau because it was an experience every tourist should have at least once. My ever-present anxiety accompanied me as usual. I was so anxious that night that most of my attention was on trying to stay calm rather than enjoying myself. On the bus ride back from the luau I became overcome with anxiety. It was so severe that I tried to swallow an anti-anxiety pill to calm me without anything to drink and it got stuck halfway down my throat. Everyone on the bus was singing 'Yellow Submarine' and I thought to myself, "Oh my gosh, I am going to die on a bus filled with a bunch of drunken tourists wearing Hawaiian shirts and singing this song!" I grabbed my wife's arm and in a faulty whisper told her I thought I was choking on my pill. She began to panic as well and urgently asked around if anyone had anything for me to drink. After everyone found out what was happening the mood quickly sobered and the singing stopped. My wife found a woman up front with a few gulps of warm soda left in her cup, so I forced the pill down with that. I had created a full blown life-or-death scene so after my crisis I slid down in my seat, utterly embarrassed. During the remainder of the trip everyone was quiet and occasionally the couple next to us looked over at me, annoyed.

Even though we were on our honeymoon and on this island paradise our arguing continued. We occasionally had moments of peace when we were distracted by the wonderful sights and exotic culture. I saw a lot of honeymooners laughing and enjoying themselves and was jealous because I was already trapped in a miserable marriage.

My unfortunate reality

When we returned from our honeymoon the arguing was even worse than before we got married. We could no longer go to our own houses though after a fight, only separate rooms. Being in a dysfunctional marriage was a major addition to the massive amount of stress I was already under from my unrelenting depression and anxiety. Because of my compounded stress I only got about three to four hours of broken sleep a night. One night as I tossed and turned my heart began beating so rapidly and forcefully that I thought I was having a heart attack. I woke my wife and told her what was happening, so she rushed me to the emergency room. After the doctor examined me he said I wasn't having a heart attack, but rather a panic attack. He explained physiologically what had occurred so if I had another one I would know what was happening. He said they are usually caused by high amounts stress; I immediately knew the sources.

I began having panic attacks regularly and I would call my doctor, instead of rushing to the

emergency room. Following are some notes from my doctor of one of my late-night phone calls.
4/30/96

"Andrew called last night (I called him at 11:30 when he was on call) and stated that "he could not slow down" and was feeling light-headed and dizzy. (I had called my doctor so many times about every kind of problem and symptom that I am sure that they were thinking, "It's the hypochondriac calling again.") Andrew presents for evaluation of panic attacks. Andrew has been seen in the office for several months and was diagnosed with situational anxiety...So far, it appears that he had tried to struggle through these symptoms with some Christian counseling, as apparently he does have a deep faith. He states that at this point, however, he is desperate, as he was unable to sleep last night feeling extremely agitated with a racing heart and some component of shortness of breath. I had a 20-minute discussion with Andrew about panic disorder and tried to emphasize to him that the current belief of panic disorder is that there is an inherent underlying biochemical imbalance in a patient who is often genetically predisposed. I have emphasized to him the importance of pharmacologic intervention, although I sensed clearly apprehension on his part to "rely on medication."

Now when I had a panic attack I no longer woke my wife, rather I laid in the dark feeling my heart pound in my chest. I started having panic attacks during the day. I was diligent in monitoring how anxious I was in public because I didn't want to have a panic attack in front of other people and them see me in such an altered mental and emotional state. The only way I could calm myself when I was overcome by my anxiety was to focus on the Lord and his Word.

Early one morning I had a severe panic attack and this time I also had a difficult time breathing. I didn't want to wake my wife so I quickly and quietly got dressed and hurried out to my car. I didn't walk too fast though because I was afraid I would use up too much oxygen and faint. My wife had previously told me there was an Urgent Care clinic nearby and it was the best place to go in an emergency because it was closer than the hospital. As I drove there I was in such a panic that I swerved on the road and went through all the red lights. When I pulled into the clinic parking lot there were no other cars because it was so early. As I anxiously waited I tried to relax and breath as slow as possible. After what seemed like a long time a car pulled up next to me with a father and son in it. The father put down his window and asked what time the clinic opened. I guess he saw the panic on my face when I answered because he looked very concerned. He asked why I was there and I told him because I was having a difficult time breathing. He urged me to get into his car right away so he could take me to the hospital. In spite of my immediate health crisis, my heart was warmed as we sped along to the hospital because this stranger cared so much that he went so far out of his way to help me.

When we arrived at the emergency room the gentleman walked me in and a nurse immediately led me back to the treatment area. The doctor examined me and said I had asthma. He gave me an inhaler and released me. When I went back out to the waiting area to thank the gracious gentleman I couldn't find him. I asked the receptionist where he was and she said to her to send him my bill and then left. I was shocked that a complete stranger had taken care of me like I was his own. I truly believe he was an angel.

I was not used to such expressions of concern as when that gentleman brought me to the hospital because I lived in a contentious atmosphere. When my wife and I fought our goal was to win the argument, instead of having a peaceful resolution. I tried to beat her by insistent reasoning and her approach was to yell over my voice. During one of our many heated exchanges I was so angry that I went to take a shower to cool-off. As I stood under the stream of water ruminating about the argument, I suddenly felt something like a vise crank down around my heart. I knew beyond a shadow of a doubt that if I didn't calm down right then I would have had a heart attack. I quickly stopped thinking about the fight and relaxed as much as I could until the pain subsided. It became crystal clear at that moment I had a serious anger problem and if I didn't deal with it right away, it would deal with me.

I never really stopped to think why I got so angry during arguments; I just said or yelled whatever hurtful or negative thoughts that came to mind. I didn't know how to stop it on my own so I decided to seek professional help. I searched the phone book for a Christian counselor and used my best discernment to select one that looked Bible-based. I was weary of selecting the right counselor because I knew there are ones who advertise they are Christian, but in reality there approach is grounded in secularism. I came across one that looked promising so I called to investigate further. When the receptionist answered I asked if their counseling was scripturally based and by her response I was confident it was, so I proceeded to make an appointment.

When I arrived for my first session I was nervous because I had never gone to Christian counseling. As I sat in the waiting area contemplating what it might be like, my counselor opened his door and invited me in. He was very kind as he introduced himself and his voice and demeanor put me at ease. He asked why I came in that day and I was hesitant to answer at first because I was afraid he might judge me like the Christians at my church did when I poured my heart out to them. I took a step of faith and began telling him about the incident in the shower when I felt like I was going to have a heart attack and that it was the impetus for me coming in. I said because of that experience I knew I had to do something to resolve my anger issue, but I didn't know what.

I told him I believed God didn't want me to get angry but no matter how hard I tried, I couldn't stop. He explained it is biblically permissible to express anger as long as I followed scriptural guidelines. He referred me to the following verses:

"Know this, my beloved brothers: let every person be quick to hear, slow to speak, slow to anger;" - James 1:19

"Be angry and do not sin; do not let the sun go down on your anger," - Ephesians 4:26

When he asked me questions about why I thought I was getting so angry my response usually started with the three same words, "I feel like...." My whole life I had mainly made my decisions on how I felt, rather than sound judgment. He told me the first step of becoming free from my uncontrolled anger is to identify the thought I had right before I got angry. He said usually the reason is outwardly apparent, but there are times when underlying issues influence the emotional response. He said to identify the root cause I needed to slow down getting angry so I could see clearly the reason why I was. I told him I had a hard time believing I had a thought right before I got angry because I usually responded so quickly. He explained that once I saw clearly what I was thinking, I could process that thought and respond in a more balanced manner.

When I started reflecting on the reasons, I stopped getting entangled in my anger emotions and saw my issues more clearly. It was difficult at first to slow down my responses when my wife and I were arguing, but it became easier the more I practiced. I became so good at it that when I saw a fight about to erupt, I was able to restrain myself from a mindless emotional response. She still yelled, but I no longer responded in an impulsive and out of control way.

My anger was in response to what I was thinking, just as with all my other emotions. God gave us emotions and they can be a great thing, just as long as they don't lead us away from the truth and good judgment. I learned to use them as a tool; like if I was anxious I knew there was something I was afraid of. I liken my emotions as lights on a car dashboard; when certain ones turned on, it could be a signal to let me know there was something wrong that I needed to look at. Not all my emotions were to alert me there was a problem though; God gave me the discernment to know if I needed to take a closer look at what was causing it, or if it was just part of my daily life. When there was something I needed to investigate further though, God gave me the wisdom to identify what was causing it and I used the tools he gave me to fix or address it. Once I dealt with the source, the light would turn off. The Lord always wants me to be aware of my 'dashboard' because it can display what is happening in me, or alert me to when a hazard may be approaching.

Even though I had dealt with my anger, our marriage continued to deteriorate. We attempted to resolve our issues on our own but no matter how hard or what we tried, nothing worked. I didn't believe in divorce so I thought the last chance to save our marriage would be Christian counseling. I was so mentally frail that I was afraid that even though we would be in a counseling session, a confrontation with her would still be too much for me to handle. Despite my fear, I asked her if she was willing to go and she said yes. Through constant prayer and reading God's Word, I maintained the courage to go.

When we arrived for our first session the counselor began by asking my wife what bothered her about our marriage. She immediately began verbally attacking me as usual and since I didn't have the mental energy to defend myself, I sank into the couch and took it. As she continued her assault the counselor told her to stop and to sit on the other side of the room. When it was my turn, I brought up the incident of how one time she stopped me from leaving the apartment when I was trying to get away from an argument. I told her I was so weak that she was able to immobilize me by wrapping her arms around me and push me against the door. My counselor asked her why she did that and she said that was how they restrained the larger animals at the veterinary clinic where she worked when they wanted to get control of them. The counselor then looked squarely at my wife and said: "He is not a dog, but a human being!" It felt so good to hear someone validate, support and protect me. She said she did not advocate divorce but because of the abuse she saw, she recommended immediate separation.

When I came home from work the following day I opened the front door and to my surprise and relief, my wife had already moved out. Because of the abrupt way she'd left the apartment felt eerily barren. Usually my cats ran to the door to greet me when I came home, but not that day. I called out to them but they still didn't come. I quickly went through the apartment looking in all their normal hiding places, but with no avail The longer I searched the more afraid I was that she had taken them. After I anxiously searched everywhere with no results, I knew my fear had come true. When I realized my best friends were gone my heart broke and I fell down sobbing in the middle of the empty dining room floor. Over the past few years while I lie sick and exhausted on the couch my cats were always there with me. Enjoying my cats company gave me a small sense of being alive and now without any warning, they were gone.

I desperately needed someone to share my grief with. I called my counselor and told him what happened and he said to come in later that day. Once I arrived at his office I shared how devastated I was because my wife took my cats. He suggested I should get two more to be my new companions (so I did). I was so thankful he was there for me in my time of need. Even though I paid him to listen and help me, I still felt he was a true friend. He sincerely cared about me and didn't judge me. I felt our friendship was the first one I had that was like what the Bible says about how brothers and sisters in Christ should treat one another.

Lies into the light

"O LORD, You have searched me and known *me*. You know when I sit down and when I rise up; You understand my thought from afar. You scrutinize my path and my lying down and are intimately acquainted with all my ways. Even before there is a word on my tongue, Behold, O LORD, You know it all." - Psalm 139:1-4

One of the worst parts of my depression was the perpetual fatigue. No matter how much physical and mental rest I got, I was still overwhelmingly exhausted. One of the many days I was too weak to get off my couch I was more depressed than usual. I was so desperate to feel even slightly better that I got up anyways to try and go out for a walk. The only thing that enabled me to get off the couch was the adrenalin created by my continual fear that I might be completely overcome by depression. When I made it outside I took a few steps and couldn't go any further, so I turned around in defeat. I went back in and fell onto my couch and began to cry. I had never truly cried before but I felt helpless to do anything else. Since I couldn't make myself feel even slightly better, I felt a deep pain that I never had before. I didn't know it was there because subconsciously whenever I felt it I would exercise to try and suppress it with the endorphins created by exercising. When I realized I had been carrying this pain for so long, I wanted to be free of it as soon possible so I decided to go back to counseling.

"The purpose in a man's heart is like deep water, but a man of understanding will draw it out."
- Proverbs 20:5

I knew the healing process could take a long time but I was determined to see it all the way through. I was going to turn over every mental and emotional rock to find anything that was stopping me from experiencing the fullness of God's love and freedom. Each counseling session we had to stay sensitive to the Holy Spirit's guidance because he was the one who gave my counselor the wisdom he needed. We dug and traveled in many directions in search of everything that was in need of mending, correction and removal. When we would come across a lie there wasn't anything the light of God's truth couldn't conquer. For example, I always thought other people were better than I. I never truly understood how valuable I was until I meditated on the following verse.

"See what kind of love the Father has given to us, that we should be called children of God; and so we are. The reason why the world does not know us is that it did not know him."
- 1 John 3:1

After we removed a lie it would often try and creep back in, so I had to vigilantly monitor my thoughts so they didn't. It wasn't uncommon to fend one off a half-dozen times after it had originally been removed. With each one we defeated I experienced a little more peace and clarity of mind.

"We destroy arguments and every lofty opinion raised against the knowledge of God and take every thought captive to obey Christ,"
- 2 Corinthians 10:5

As well as my thoughts being transformed by God's truths, my heart needed to be set free from all the hurt that weighed it down. If my heart wasn't mended, my healing wouldn't have been complete. I had forgotten most of the events that caused my pain, but the damage they inflicted remained. My heart was full of tears and anger and it all needed to be released. Since God had shown me how to open my heart, my tears and anger were now free to flow out. I released some of the pain during counseling, but most of it when I wasn't.

Most of my pain would unpredictably come to the surface when I wasn't thinking about much. Whenever I felt like I needed to cry it didn't matter if I was in private or public, I didn't hold back the tears like I always had. If I was in public and I needed to, I would find a place out of sight so I could. As far as releasing my anger, I would have to wait until I got home to. The way I let it out was to either punch or yell into my pillows. Sometimes I got so angry that I had to stack up extra pillows so I wouldn't hurt my knuckles when I punched them.

After approximately a year of talking about past issues and releasing tears and anger, I felt free from most of my past destructive thoughts and emotions. I was now able to settle into a daily maintenance mode of facing any new negative thoughts and emotions the way God taught me to.

"for wisdom will come into your heart and knowledge will be pleasant to your soul;"
- Proverbs 2:10

"And I will give you a new heart and a new spirit I will put within you. And I will remove the heart of stone from your flesh and give you a heart of flesh." - Ezekiel 36:26

God gave me the victory over my mental and emotional pain, but my daily spiritual battle raged on. One night as I read my Bible I had a very sinful thought and I believed it was so bad that God would never forgive me of it. I was so horrified of being separated from God for eternity that I flew into a full-blown panic attack and drove as fast as I could to my church to find my pastor. As soon as I pulled into the church parking lot I jumped out and ran in. A wedding ceremony had just finished and I saw my pastor sitting in a pew visiting with a guest. I went over and interrupted their conversation and told him

I was desperate to talk with him. He excused himself and we went to a back pew so we could talk in private. I told him what happened and that I was afraid God wouldn't forgive me. He opened his Bible and showed me the following verses:

"If we confess our sins, he is faithful and just to forgive us our sins and to cleanse us from all unrighteousness." - 1 John 1:9

"And you, who were dead in your trespasses and the uncircumcision of your flesh, God made alive together with him, having forgiven us all our trespasses," - Colossians 2:13

He explained that God had already forgiven me for all my sins, past, present and future. As soon as he showed me those verses and explained the full implications of what Jesus had already done for me on the cross, a wave of peace came over me and my panic subsided. I thanked him greatly and casually strolled back to my car. My fear was gone for a few days, but unfortunately returned. I started thinking my pastor's answer was too simple; I believed there must be a loophole somewhere in Scripture to what he stated. My uncertainty put terror in my heart because as a Christian, I now knew the unimaginable consequences of not having all my sins forgiven. My thoughts began to continually race and heart trembled because I felt I was always riding on the edge of God's acceptance or rejection.

I became obsessed with finding more verses that supported what my pastor said about how God forgave me all my sins. I delved deep into Scripture and found many verses that supported what my pastor said and some that seemed like they didn't. The belief that God will never leave those who have already asked him for forgiveness is referred to as 'eternal security.' I scoured the Bible daily, studied multiple resources and asked many Christians what they thought about this subject, but never got a satisfactory answer. About a year after I initially brought this issue to my pastor I went back and told him I was still struggling with his answer. He told me I should stop fixating on finding possible cracks in the Scripture he originally referred to and focus on what Jesus had already done for me on the cross. I understood what he was saying but even though it was a solid answer, I still felt it didn't give me the concrete answer I was looking for. I continued my obsession on trying to find the exact verse(s) that would wipe away all doubt of me not being eternally secure.

No matter what I was doing, the terror I might be separated from God was always just under the surface; it even often woke me at night. The only thing that gave me enough peace to go back to sleep was reading my Bible. I had to read in the bathroom though because if I turned on the light anywhere else, it would wake my wife. About a year of battling this fear I went to the bathroom one night to read and I was so weak I couldn't even sit up, so I laid on the floor and put my head down next to my Bible. I had completely exhausted myself mentally and physically trying to find out if I could ever lose my salvation with no avail. In total desperation I cried out from the depths of my heart, "Please don't leave me Lord!" The moment those words fell from my lips I heard God say in a gentle voice, "I am never going to leave you." and immediately I felt my massive fear lifted.

"Trust in the LORD with all your heart And do not lean on your own understanding."
-Proverbs 3:5

That night I learned how to trust the Lord with the deepest burden of my heart. I straight away began bringing all my burdens to Him but it was difficult at first because I was used to 'handling' my problems on my own. I soon learned to not hesitate to bring them to Him because I was too weak to try and carry them. The longer I cast my cares upon Him, the more I relied on his strength and not mine. If I hadn't brought my troubles to the Lord, I know I wouldn't have survived my depression.

"casting all your anxieties on him, because he cares for you." - 1 Peter 5:7

When I asked God to forgive me for my sins I entered into a spiritual relationship with him, but soon after I subconsciously began to not trust him. In my head I knew God is love, but I was still afraid he might hurt me just like everyone else in my life had; so I tried to push him away to protect myself. He wanted me to draw close to Him in my heart so he allowed the storm of the fear I might lose my salvation to pound against me until I either reached out to him to rescue me, or let myself be overcome by it. When the moment of decision arrived and I choose the Lord, the torment that God allowed had accomplished its purpose.

Learning how to truly open my heart to the Lord was just the beginning of my intimate walk with him. Just as with any other relationship, it took time for me to trust and love him more. The more I shared with the Lord the closer I felt; I didn't reveal all myself though at once, it was a slow process. Since the Lord knew I had a difficult time trusting people in the past, he understood my trepidation. He told me that just because my progression to trust him more was slow, he still required me to push forward daily and to never turn back. Even though it was very difficult at times, I continued to open up in faith. Sometimes when I was praying and felt myself putting up my shield, I kept my heart open by focusing on God's character rather than my fears of the past. I focused on the following verses and they reassured me that He was safe and wouldn't hurt me.

"Anyone who does not love does not know God, because *God is love.*" - 1 John 4:8

"Love is patient and kind; love does not envy or boast; it is not arrogant or rude. It does not insist on its own way; it is not irritable or resentful; it does not rejoice at wrongdoing, but rejoices with the truth. Love bears all things, believes all things, hopes all things, endures all things." - 1 Corinthians 4-7

Solitary world

After my wife left me I was alone, except for the Lord; His presence and our close relationship comforted and sustained me. All of my thoughts and energy now focused on the Lord and my mental and emotional battle. I began pulling away from the people and places around me because I felt like I no longer fit in. My urge was to isolate myself, but I still forced myself to get out of my apartment, no matter how I felt or weak I was.

My apartment was in an old Quaker farmhouse house that had been converted into apartments. The house was surrounded by large untilled crop fields and there was a barn outback. One day I was exploring the barn and found a rusted horseshoe under some matted down leaves. I got the idea to play a game of horseshoes with it so I searched around for something I could use as the post. I found an old rusty pipe and went and pushed it into the ground where I was going to play. I walked back to where I thought the proper throwing distance was, turned and tossed the horseshoe as close to the pipe as I could. I slowly trudged back and forth through the wet leaves as I threw and fetched the horseshoe. Playing this game by myself made me think about how prisoners must feel when they are in solitary confinement. Being separated from other inmates is almost always temporary, unlike depression which can entrap a person indefinitely.

Something else that helped me get out was gardening. I got permission from my landlord to make a garden on the property so I searched the grounds and found a small, suitable patch of grass next to the house. The area was on a slope so I made a three-tier garden with bricks I'd found. Once it was constructed and the soil prepared; I planted tomatoes, lettuce, peas and broccoli. I diligently tended to it and inspected each plant daily to see how much it had grown since the day before. I enjoyed watching them grow because it reminded me there was still life in the world. When they eventually yielded their vegetables, I enjoyed every fresh bite throughout the growing season.

When I went out the thing I enjoyed most was going to a nearby park. It was about half-mile away and when the weather was good I walked over. When I was home all I did was sleep and lay on the couch so I forced myself to walk there, no matter how fatigued I was.; it was worth the struggle though because it was the only thing that helped lift my spirits. My favorite place was on a bridge that spanned the large pond there. I spent much of my time standing in the middle of that bridge watching the large orange carp and ducks swim around and under it. On the other side of the pond was where visitors went to feed the ducks. I didn't venture over to where they were though because I was alone so much that I had become uncomfortable around people. One day as I approached the bridge I saw a father and son fishing from the spot where I usually stood. I didn't want to disturb them so I stayed off the bridge. As I watched them from the bank I envied their relationship and time together because my parents divorced when I was very young and I rarely saw my father.

Because I had an increasingly difficult time being around people I rarely went to church. I read my Bible and prayed daily, but I still desired to be around other Christians. The few times I was brave enough to go, I was always on the verge of a panic attack and had to continually fight my urge to run out. One of the few times I made it through an entire service I met a friendly couple and they invited me over for dinner. I was excited about the invitation but anxious at the same time because I hadn't been in a social situation for a long time and was worried my behavior might seem a little 'off'. I was afraid I wouldn't be able to escape if I felt overwhelmed by anxiety. I also wasn't sure if I would have the mental endurance to have an extended visit. Despite my anxieties, I was determined to go.

The evening arrived when it was time to go over for dinner and I prayed for the Lord to calm my heart and give me the mental and physical strength to have an enjoyable time. When I arrived I was pleasantly surprised when the whole family greeted me at the door. Their home was meagerly furnished and it was obvious they didn't have a lot of money, but it seemed it didn't matter because there was a lot of love there. The couple and I visited while the kids played in one of their bedrooms. I enjoyed hearing the children because they were full of life and joy.

When dinner was ready we all sat down at the kitchen table. I was eager to start because at home I usually ate the same bland foods every day. I savored each bite that night because I wasn't sure if I would ever taste a home-cooked meal again. After we finished we retired back to the living room to visit a while longer; I was glad I had the mental endurance to do so. At the end of the evening I didn't want to leave because I had to return to my dark and solitary world.

Even though my visit was a success, I was still afraid to be around people. I tried to avoid crowds as much as possible, but I couldn't when I went to the grocery store. As I shopped I would pray for the Lord to keep me calm enough so I wouldn't run out and leave my groceries behind. I knew this fear was irrational so I went to the library to research what may be happing to me. I learned I developed agoraphobia. Agoraphobia is defined in the Merriam Webster dictionary as: "An abnormal fear of being helpless in a situation from which escape may be difficult or embarrassing that is characterized initially often by panic or anticipatory anxiety and finally by the avoidance of open or public places." Because of my fear I was becoming increasingly more withdrawn from society and I knew I had to do something about it before it got any worse. Determined not to let this fear take over, I often recited the following verse:

"for God gave us a spirit not of fear but of power and love and self-control." - 2 Timothy 1:7

I thought going to a movie would be a good place to begin pushing against my isolating behaviors. I felt this was a good place to start because it was a dark and controlled environment and my contact with others would be limited. I went one evening and before I got out of the car I saw my first challenge was to walk across the parking lot to the ticket window. After I got out of the car I prayed each step of the way until I got to the window. I was so excited when I reached it because I had overcome my first obstacle of the evening. After I had bought my ticket, I went in and found where my movie was playing. As I stood in the entrance of the theater I scanned all the rows multiple times to find the exact seat I thought I would feel the safest in. Once I decided on a seat I went and sat down. Almost immediately my panic tried to take control and I felt like running out, so I literally held onto my seat. I was determined not to be controlled by my fear so the more intense it became, the harder I prayed. After battling it for a while I became calm enough to be able to start enjoying the movie. Occasionally during the film my anxiety tried to rear its ugly head again, but I quickly prayed it away. I enjoyed the rest of the movie and once it ended, I was thrilled because I had taken my first step against my agoraphobia.

Around the same time I became increasingly anxious the further away I drove from my apartment. When I would be driving I felt like there was a large rubber band around my waist and the further I drove, the more the tension increased. I would pray for the Lord to keep me calm enough so I wouldn't get in an accident. If I became too anxious I pulled off to the side of the road and read some verses from a small Bible I always carried with me. I wrote down so many helpful verses on the front and back pages of it that my writing became almost microscopic. Once I reached my destination I would quickly do what I needed to and then drive right back. The closer I drove to my home the more the tension decreased.

The radius around my house where I felt safe to drive got increasing smaller until one day I was nervous to even get into my car. I knew I had to do something about it before I was too frightened to drive at all. I thought a way to fight this fear was to take a drive each day and go a little further out than I had the day before. The first few times I could only drive a few blocks more at a time before I was too anxious to go any further. Every day when I got to the edge of where I went the day before, I prayed for the Lord to keep me safe as I crossed the next imaginary boundary. I traveled further each day and after about a month I was able to drive halfway across the state. When I was able to drive that far I was no longer worried about being confined by this fear. This triumph was pivotal because it stopped my agoraphobia from making my world spiral in on itself.

Job after job

Over the four years my depression was the most severe I had a difficult time keeping a job. I always had to work though because I had no other way to support myself. I was continually mentally and physically exhausted and it took much more effort for me to complete the same tasks as other employees. I tried to find shortcuts and workarounds so I could do the most possible with the least amount of energy. Most of the time I knew my coworkers resented me because I wasn't doing as much as they were. Asking me to do the same quality and quantity of work though was like asking me to lift a thousand pounds, which of course I couldn't, no matter how hard I tried or wanted to. At each job I knew I wasn't a good employee but I tried to keep up the appearance as long as I could. The reasons why I left each job fluctuated between being fired because of my poor performance and quitting because the duties were too difficult.

The first job I had when I moved back to Schenectady was at a daycare facility for the mentally disabled. The purpose of the facility was to give clients the skills they needed to be gainfully employed. One day as I ate lunch with my coworkers my thoughts began wondering aimlessly. I was very frightened because nothing like this had ever happened to me before. I went back inside to try and gather my thoughts and figure out what was going on. After about fifteen minutes I was able to gain control of my thoughts again. This incident made me aware I was having some mental health problems, but I had to put my fears aside and continue pushing ahead in life.

My depression caused me to have a very negative attitude, so my coworkers normally didn't want to talk with, or be around me. I tried my hardest not to offend anyone so they would like me; but no matter what I said or did though nothing changed. I didn't know how poor my attitude was until one day when my boss called me into his office. He said the other employees were complaining about how hard it was to work with me. He said they didn't feel comfortable enough to approach me about it themselves because they weren't sure how I would react. When he told me this it saddened me deeply because I was trying to get along with everyone the best I could. I wasn't aware I had such a bad attitude because my depression kept me from seeing my negativity. I was so brokenhearted about the situation that I quit right then.

Impulsively quitting my job was not a wise decision because I didn't have enough money to pay the following months rent. Since my degree was in education I thought being a substitute teacher would be a quick solution to my financial situation. I thought it would also be a good fix because if I didn't feel well on any given day I could stay home without fearing any negative repercussions from a principle. I applied at the district office and received my first substitute teacher request a couple days later. Almost all of the requests came from the same three middle schools that were in the worst part of the city. No substitutes wanted to go to them because the students were very disrespectful. I accepted most requests from those schools though because I needed the money. Substitutes didn't earn much to begin with and working at those schools made the pay even less compensatory. From when I first entered the classroom in those difficult schools in the morning, until the end of the day, I was a continual target for the student's amusement.

I was a young Christian when I started substituting and still wasn't sure how to express my emotions in a way that I thought was honoring to God. I still believed a 'good Christian' shouldn't express or display any anger or displeasure. Because of my erroneous belief I tried to keep a smile on no matter how poorly the students treated me and how I felt. Because I didn't know how to deal with my anger, it built up the longer I worked there.

One day as I taught an art class a student shot a water gun at me and I held in my anger as usual. This time when I did, my chest tightened and I had a difficult time breathing. I thought I was having a heart attack so I called the school nurse and she said to come right down. I was only twenty-seven at the time but I felt like seventy as I shuffled slowly down the hall. As kids walked by they stared and by the looks on their faces I could tell they were thinking something like, "What is wrong with that guy!?" After what seemed like much longer than it actually was, I finally arrived at the nurse's office. She took my vital signs and said they were fine. When I heard the results I relaxed and my heart rate slowed. She asked if I wanted her to call an ambulance but I said no because I was beginning to feel better. Because of that incident, I never substituted again.

Since I was a teacher and also liked helping people, I wanted my next job to be a combination of what I liked to do. I searched the classifieds and found a listing for a crew leader for the mentally ill. I thought this position would be good for me so I applied and was hired. My main duty was to take a group of about eight mentally ill individuals out into the community and give them direction during house cleaning and yard maintenance jobs. In addition to my supervisory duties I was also supposed to assist when needed. My manager often had a hard time finding work for us because of the client's limitations. When she couldn't find anything she contacted the city because they always had some work for us. She didn't like asking them though because they always offered us work that their employees didn't like to do themselves.

Some of the work they gave us was to clean up around the abandoned houses in a run-down part of the city. That area had a reputation of being violent and drug infested. Many people thought twice about driving thru there, even during the day. One time when I pulled up in front of one of the houses we had to clean around, we let out a collective sigh because of all the garbage we saw piled up around it. The sky was gray and it was drizzling, which made the task in front of us seem that much more awful. Because there was so much garbage, I knew I had to help. Since I was the supervisor I chose first where I was going to work and I decided on the area in the back of the house because it looked like there was the least amount of trash there.

I was wet and miserable as I worked and tried not to smell or think about what I was picking up. I was only wearing shorts and a t-shirt so the longer I picked up trash, the more filth clung to my arms and legs. Because of my perpetual fatigue I became tired shortly after I started, so I went back to the van to get a drink of water and rest a bit. As I leaned against the van I looked up at the gray sky and reflected on how horrible my life had become. When I was younger I could have never imagined that my life would have been reduced to this. I looked around at the neighborhood full of debris and decay and reflected on how my life felt like how these surroundings looked.

When I drove home at the end of each day I was so exhausted that I often could barely focus on the road. I didn't have an ounce of physical or mental energy left from the ounce I started the day with. When I got back I would even have a difficult time walking up the stairs to my apartment. My heart was so stressed that it felt like a taut balloon and with every step up I took I was afraid it might explode. Since I had no choice but to walk up the stairs, I had to face this fear. I would stand at the bottom of the stairs and look up and wonder if I was going to make it to the top alive. I would pray "Lord, I am putting my life in your hands with every step I take." I would raise my foot onto the first step and then slowly bring up the other. When both feet were on the first step I would breathe a sigh of relief and then continue up to the next. For a healthy person it would have taken about five seconds to walk up the flight of stairs, but for me it took about five minutes. I knew Christians had to walk by faith and I chuckled one time as I thought about how literally that applied to this situation. Climbing those steps daily helped me trust the Lord more with my life.

"Therefore, being always of good courage and knowing that while we are at home in the body we are absent from the Lord—for we walk by faith, not by sight." - 2 Corinthians 5: 6-7

I became so mentally and physically weak that at work I had a difficult time performing my job duties. Most times when the crew needed my help I avoided it by staying in the van pretending I was doing important supervisory paperwork. I knew they probably didn't buy my act but they didn't say anything because I was the supervisor. After a few months I felt they started complaining to my supervisor because her attitude changed towards me and she began scrutinizing my work. One day she came to a job with me to observe my performance. When we were about halfway through I sat down next to her on a bench and told her I was too tired to work. I said I had to find somewhere else to work that wasn't as physically demanding. She asked why I didn't tell her sooner and I said that I was too ashamed.

The next place I worked was at a gift shop in a nearby airport. I felt my job was menial and I was embarrassed to ring-up customers in my cheap blue vest. One day as I straightened the magazines in front I saw my old girlfriend from high school, Susan; she also worked at the airport. I was very self-conscious because I knew I looked disheveled and a sad reflection of the person she used to know. Even though I wasn't confident with my appearance or proud of my life, I was so desperate for human interaction that I put on a big fake smile and walked over to say hello. When we greeted she gave me a polite hug and asked what I had been doing since high school. I was so embarrassed by how sick I was and what my life had been reduced to that I mainly shared about my successes in college and then quickly redirected the question back to her. Since we both worked at the airport we decided to continue our conversation over lunch.

We went to a nearby deli and Susan got a nice salad and I took out my peanut butter and jelly sandwich from my brown lunch bag. As we ate we had a nice time reminiscing about high school, but we gradually ran out of things to reflect on. As we continued we talked more about our current lives and the longer we did I became increasingly self-conscious; I felt she might be noticing my slightly scattered thoughts and depressed mood. We soon finished our meals and said our goodbyes.

The next day I saw Susan staring at me from a restaurant across the hall from the gift ship. I believed she was staring because she was perplexed at how different I had become. I acted like I didn't see her and continued on with my job duties. My landlord stopped by the gift shop to say hello because he was just killing time waiting for his friend's flight to arrive. I didn't have any friends and he was one of the few people I knew. As we talked I exaggerated my laughter and smiles to make it appear like we were good friends. I wanted her to think I was the same 'confident' person I projected I was in high school. After he left I still felt her eyes on me so I quickly turned my head towards her to confront her stare and she quickly looked away. I was so embarrassed by how ill I had become that from then on whenever I saw her I tried to hide. I didn't work there much longer because I was fired for calling in sick too often.

The next place I worked was at a convenience store. I had a minimal amount of job duties such as making coffee and stocking milk in the cooler, so most of my time was spent just standing behind the cash register. There were a couple regular customers who broke up the monotony and I always looked forward to seeing them. When either one of them were there we would joke around and I actually had some fun! Over the few months I worked there we became friends and I even went to one of their houses a couple times. They were my only social contact and they briefly distracted me from my depression.

The only life I had was at work, so I didn't mind going in whenever they needed help. One day they asked if anyone wanted to work Christmas Eve and I volunteered. On Christmas Eve my coworkers were excited and full of anticipation because they were looking forward to the evening celebrations. At the end of their shifts they joyfully said Merry Christmas to me as they walked out the door. I didn't like working alone but I was thankful to be at the store though, instead of being trapped alone in my apartment with my depressive thoughts and anxiety. Hardly anyone came in that night so I spent most of my time looking out the window watching the snow fall. Occasionally a customer came in to buy milk or other essentials and then rush back out. It snowed heavily most of that evening and quickly everything was under a thick white blanket. The snow was mostly undisturbed except for some tire tracks on the road from people who were brave enough to venture out into the cold.

As I thought about all the families being together and enjoying themselves, I told the Lord how terribly alone I felt. Soon after I prayed the little bell on the front door rang and my heart jumped as I saw one of my favorite customers walk in. He told me while he was eating dinner with his family he thought of me and that I might enjoy some of their Christmas dinner. He handed me a tinfoil covered plate and I joyfully accepted it. I told him how deeply I appreciated his thoughtfulness. We talked a while and then he said he had to get back. He wished me a merry Christmas as he went out into the snowy night. The thing I appreciated most about the meal was that my friend thought enough about me to bear the cold and snow to bring it to me. I no longer felt alone and I thanked the Lord for the tremendous blessing.

I was getting to know most of the customers and the longer I worked there the more I felt like part of the community. I was enjoying my routine of going to work and visiting with the customers. As I got ready to go in one day the store manager called and told me the money count was a hundred dollars short and he accused me of stealing it. I was adamant I hadn't taken it because there was no way I would jeopardize my job. He didn't want to hear anything I said and he fired me right then. I was shocked and brokenhearted because the little pleasure and distraction from my misery was taken away. Once again, I had to find another job.

As I searched through the classifieds I came across a listing for a food court worker at a local mall. Before my illness I would've been too proud to even consider such a job, but now I would feel even fortunate to get it. When I called to enquire about the position they told me I could come in and fill out an application. When I went in the following day I completed my application and the receptionist directed me to the maintenance manager's office. When I entered, to my great surprise, my friend from high school was sitting behind the desk! His name was Greg and we weren't that close in school but he was one of the few people who was genuinely nice to me. I was now a college graduate and should have had a successful professional career by then, but I stood humbly before him hoping to be hired. We were glad to see one another and we visited and shared about what we had been doing since high school. Just as with Susan, I tried to skim over the specifics of my life and focus on his. Even though our conversation was casual, the whole time in the back of my mind I was still trying to portray myself as a competent employee. I think Greg had already made up his mind to hire me the moment I walked in, so when he offered me the position it seemed like just a formality.

My main job duty was to stand in the food court waiting for people to finish their meals so I could clean their table after they left. I was very embarrassed performing this type of work, especially in front of so many people. I had to swallow my pride though if I wanted to get a paycheck. My first duty in the morning before my day in the food court began was to empty the cigarette butt cans throughout the mall and clean the glass entrance doors and windows. I had become so weak by then that it was even difficult for me to raise my arms high enough over my head to clean the top parts of the windows. All my coworkers were stronger than I, including a sixty-year-old coworker. She could throw three bags of trash into the dumpster in the same time it took me to feebly lift in one. Even though I was so weak, I still had to force myself to finish each day.

One morning as I performed my cleaning ritual I became so dizzy that I had to sit down. Greg happened to be walking down the hall towards me and when he reached me I told him how I felt. I asked him to call the ambulance if I fainted. I think he thought I was joking because he lightheartedly agreed. I relaxed as we talked because I knew if something happened he was right there to help. I frequently worried if I was going to faint and would pray to help fight off the anxiety. Always praying to combat my fears was a major contributor to helping me draw closer to the Lord.

The mall was near where I'd grown up so I was nervous that someone I knew would see me working there. One day an old girlfriend from high school, Darlene, was walking down the hall towards me. I didn't treat her well when we were dating and always had one eye on other girls. I broke up with her because I thought I could do better. By the time I saw her she was so close that meeting face-to-face was inevitable. Because of how poorly I treated her, I felt like pulling my shirt over my head. When she reached me we said hello and I started the conversation by asking how she had been. She told me she had a wonderful husband and that they had bought a nice house close to where we grew up. Now, fourteen years later she had a full life and all I had was a cleaning bottle in one hand and my shame and humiliation in the other.

One day when I was just hanging out in Greg's office he got a call on his handset that a toilet was overflowing in one of the men's restrooms. Since I was right there he gave me the honor and showed me where the plunger was. I had many humbling experiences when I worked there and this one was at the top of the list. The men's room was on the other side of the mall so I had to walk the entire length of it with my big blue plunger in hand. As I weaved my way through the crowds I didn't make eye contact with anyone and just focused on my destination. I often wished I was invisible when I worked there and this was definitely one of those times. Once I reached the bathroom and cleaned up I prayed for the courage to help me overcome my embarrassment on the way back. At that moment the following verse came to mind:

"The fear of the LORD is instruction in wisdom and *humility comes before honor.*"
- Proverbs 15:33

After a few months of working at the mall I could no longer summons the strength to complete my job duties, so I quit.

My annual income had been approximately nine thousand dollars for the previous three years and I'd always managed to just get by. Since I quit I couldn't pay the following months rent and being homeless became a real possibility. This fear pounded louder in me with each passing day so I turned to God's Word for comfort. I learned that putting my complete faith in Him was the only way to keep from drowning in my worries and fears. I knew God would provide for me but I still needed verses to hold onto for hope. I searched the Bible and God directed me to the following verses:

"Therefore do not be anxious, saying, 'What shall we eat?' or 'What shall we drink?' or 'What shall we wear?' For the Gentiles seek after all these things and your heavenly Father knows that you need them all. But seek first the kingdom of God and his righteousness and all these things will be added to you. Therefore do not be anxious about tomorrow, for tomorrow will be anxious for itself. Sufficient for the day is its own trouble." - Matthew 6:31-34

"do not be anxious about anything, but in everything by prayer and supplication with thanksgiving let your requests be made known to God. And the peace of God, which surpasses all understanding, will guard your hearts and your minds in Christ Jesus." - Philippians 4:6-7

A few days before my rent was due I got a call out of the blue from my friend who had brought me dinner that Christmas Eve at the convenience store. He was the property manager of a government subsidized apartment complex and he knew how much financially I was struggling. One of the apartments had opened up and he asked me if I was interested. I first said "Heck yeah!" and then "Praise God!" I told him I didn't have a job and hardly any money and he said that wasn't a problem because if I didn't have an income the rent was only twenty-five dollars a month! I knew God provided me the apartment and after I got off the phone I ran around my living room with my hands in the air thanking and praising God. That miracle took a tremendous burden off me. I was also so thankful because I was becoming weaker every day and I didn't know how much longer I would be able to work. I was now comforted by the fact that when I was unable to support myself anymore that at least I would have a place to live.

I hired a moving van with some of the little money I had left. When the movers arrived I tried to help but I was so weak that I was essentially useless; I only had the strength to pick up some couch pillows and a couple lampshades. I was learning to accept my physical limitations but it was still difficult to stop exerting myself beyond what I was capable of doing. I was glad I was leaving that apartment because of all the mental and physical suffering I endured there. I thought living in a new apartment and area would help put me on a path of healing and happiness. I wouldn't have been able to bear the knowledge though of what I was about to live through.

Edge of death

"I am utterly bowed down and prostrate; all the day I go about mourning." - Psalm 38:6

I was already familiar with the apartment complex where I was moving to because I had grown up in the suburbs about five miles away from it. I had gone there once with a friend and wanted to leave as soon as possible because I thought it was where the 'dysfunctional' part of society lived. I was so proud that I thought the only way I would be around 'people like these' was for charitable reasons. It was ironic that the place I was so quick to get away from as a teenager, was where I was now grateful to live.

When the movers arrived at my new place and began unloading I once again felt guilty for not being able to help; all I could do was stand off to the side and watch them do all the work. Even though I was frustrated I couldn't help, I was learning to accept my limitations. After they finished and left I stood alone in my living room amongst the pile of my possessions; I then looked at the challenge ahead and began to unpack my things.

Once I settled in I found a job at a sandwich shop just down the road. As always my coworkers were the only people I had any regular contact with. Even though we worked side-by-side we didn't interact much. We were physically in the same location but inside we were worlds apart. They joked around and talked about their lives but once again, I felt like an outsider looking in. If I did partake of their conversations though all I would have been able to contribute was that I was always alone, severely exhausted, suffering from mental and emotional torment and constantly struggling to stay sane and alive.

Almost every night after the other employees had left a homeless man came in for dinner. I recognized him because I had seen him many times on the streets pushing his shopping-cart around the city collecting cans. When he came in he always parked his cart directly outside the store window where he sat so he could keep a close eye on the fruits of his hard day of labor. I was uncomfortable around him because of his lack of hygiene, tattered clothes and that he sifted through trash all day. After serving him regularly for about two weeks though, I started striking up conversations with him while I prepared his meals. I thought we both didn't have anyone to talk with so we mutually enjoyed our conversations. His thoughts were scattered and it appeared like he had schizophrenia; but that didn't matter because I didn't have the mental energy to have a very substantive conversation as well. I thought I was ministering to him by trying to be a friend, but it turned out he was ministering to me in the same way. He was the only person I talked with on a regular basis and I always looked forward to seeing him. I was well groomed and appeared healthy on the outside, but inside this homeless man and I were both fighting our own ugly mental illness.

Before I closed the store each night I had my list of duties to perform such as putting the food away in the cooler, washing dishes and mopping the floors. One night as I performed my closing routine my heart was suddenly filled with overwhelming pain; I was surprised at it because I wasn't thinking about much at the time. I felt a wave of tears whelm up in me and it was so intense that I knew I had to get off my feet, so I sat on a food prep table. The tears began to flow and I curled up into a ball on the table because the pain was so intense. As I sobbed I had a flashback to when I was four and my mother and father sat all of us kids down at the kitchen table and told us dad wasn't going to be living with us anymore. At the time I didn't understand they were getting a divorce, I just felt extremely sad and confused. This memory was so intense that it was the only one I had remembered from when I was that young. After crying on that table for about fifteen minutes I felt the largest release of pain I ever had.

I experienced tremendous amounts of healing in my heart and mind through counseling, prayer and endless hours of introspection during my years of solitary depression. Even though I gained an immense amount of mental and emotional healing, my brain had been physically damaged from all the years of overwhelming stress put on it by my illness. I felt my ability to process information was impeded and I thought I was losing touch with reality. To discern what was real or not, I used the Bible as my guide. If I didn't have Scripture to refer to and direct me, I would have easily lost my mental bearings and would have been perpetually confused. Because of my poor mental condition I cannot remember much of what happened to me during this time in my life; but following are some poignant experiences I can recall well enough to record.

Pushing through the Snow

Since exercise was the only thing that slightly helped stave off my depression, I walked or jogged relentlessly every day for over the three years my depression was the worst. Since I never rested from 'exercising', my body wasn't being strengthened but rather being broken down. I was sacrificing my body for the energy to fight my mental battle. I was always so weak that I got cold easily and it was the worst when I slept. To try and stay warm at night I kept the thermostat at eighty, wore multiple layers of cloths and slept under a pile of blankets. Despite my efforts to keep warm, I was woken one night by an awful feeling that my core body temperature had dropped. To try and warm myself I knew I had to get my heart pounding to increase my circulation, so I frantically put on my layers of winter clothes and went out to jog.

My destination was a small hill a few blocks away. I'd discovered it was the best place to jog because the incline was just steep enough to quickly increase my heart rate, without putting too much strain on it. There had been a large snowstorm earlier that night and the only place clear enough to walk was in the middle of the road. It was especially quiet because it was in the middle of the night and any ambient noise was dampened by the freshly fallen snow. As I walked I watched the snowflakes fall from the grayish white sky and be illuminated as they passed under the streetlights.

When I got to the bottom of the hill the snow was so deep that I knew all I could do was try and walk up it. My legs were so weak that they felt like dead wood; so I had to fight to lift up each leg and slowly lunge my way through the deep snow. As usual, the only thing that kept my spirits from being crushed was talking with the Lord and feeling His presence. As I pushed upwards a police car rolled up next to me and the officer waved me over. He asked what I was doing and I said I was exercising. He looked at me puzzled, but my answer seemed to satisfy his curiosity enough that he drove off. Considering I was walking up and down this snow covered hill in the middle of the night, I would have done the same thing if I were him. Sometimes I had to do things that helped me fight my depression; even though they might have appeared odd to those around me. After a short while of trudging through the snow I felt warmer so I went back home.

One of my many trips to the Emergency Room

One evening when I was watching television I suddenly had a difficult time breathing. I tried my inhaler a few times but it didn't work so I called 911. I had gone to the emergency room so many times that I knew I had to remain calm because panicking didn't help. When the paramedics arrived I was too short of breath to get off my couch so I called out for them to come in. After they examined me they determined I should go to the hospital. I was very embarrassed as they wheeled me out on the gurney because a petite female medic was holding the foot of it as they took me down the stairs, out of the building, over a snow bank and into the ambulance. I used to be proud of how physically fit I was, but this experience made it blatantly clear to me how much my youthful strength was a thing of the past.

Once I arrived at the ER they put me in a room by myself and adhered EKG wires to my chest. As I lie there alone all I could do was watch my heart rate activity on the cardiac monitor and listen to the beep of my heart rate. As I patiently waited for the doctor I was still scared, but I focused on the Lord to help keep me from panicking. His still small voice in me reassured me that he was right there and in complete control. While I fought to stay emotionally in control I worried that if I died no one I knew would be there and the only thing they would write on my chart would be 'Inform relatives.' I prayed the whole time and in about fifteen minutes my breathing returned to normal so they released me.

Outside Looking In

One night when I had to go out for a walk it was especially cold. The freezing gusts of wind were so strong that I stayed within the confines of the apartment complex so the buildings would shield me. My face quickly became numb and I curled up my fingers into the middle of my gloves to try and keep them warm. I felt especially alone as I passed by the darkened windows because I knew most of the tenants were tucked in for the night, deep in slumber. I came to an apartment that was dimly lit by a television in the living room. Standing out in the cold and darkness and looking in at the faint dancing images on the walls, intensified my feelings of being alone in the world.

Demise of the ability to support myself

I quit my job at the sandwich shop because I didn't get along well with my coworkers and boss. I once again scoured the classifieds and came across a listing for someone to work at a group home for the mentally and physically disabled. I was immediately interested in the position because I worked at a group home when I lived in California and I knew how easy it could be. The position was also appealing because the clients would be far worse off mentally than I so I wouldn't be self-conscious about any peculiar mannerisms I might display. I applied for the job and was hired.

Just as I predicted my duties were light. They consisted of helping clients with their hygiene, making sure they took their medications, helping maintain the house and supervise the clients during activities. I was so weak though that I had a difficult time even accomplishing my minimal amount of duties. I spent a lot of time on the couch watching television with the clients and the least amount of time off of it. I knew my coworkers resented me because I didn't do my share of the work. I felt bad I couldn't do more, but I was just too weak to.

The longer I 'worked' there the more my depression continued feeding on whatever was left of me. Mentally and physically I was almost totally consumed and I obsessed on the fear that my body could completely shut down at any moment. One night a coworker and I were watching television and I suddenly felt my heart weaken. I was petrified it was going to stop so I quickly got up and told my coworker I was going out to get some fresh air; I am sure he thought what I was doing was peculiar because a dense fog had just settled in and it had begun to lightly rain. I wasn't dressed to go out in that weather, but I did anyways.

I started a very feeble 'jog' on the steep part of the road in front of the house. I thought how odd I must have looked to people in passing by cars because I was jogging in the rain wearing my regular clothes and no jacket. After about ten minutes I felt my heart pumping stronger so I went back in. I was soaked as I entered the living room and my coworker looked at me like "What is wrong with this guy?" I knew he was baffled by my behavior but I walked by him with no explanation. I didn't have anything dry to change into, so I went down into the basement where the washer and dryer where to get some of the clients freshly laundered cloths.

I found some sweatpants and a t-shirt and when I was putting on the dry cloths I saw a client on the stairwell looking down at me. Even though he was mentally disabled, I could see on his face that he instinctively sensed something was unusual about what I was doing. He became uncomfortable so he did what he always did when he felt like that; scream and hit his head. He ran upstairs and I followed him to try and calm him down, but he escaped to his bedroom. I went back into the living room and quickly made up an excuse to my coworker about why I thought the client was upset. I sat down on the couch and tried to appear like nothing out of the ordinary had occurred.

One day when I was watching television with the clients and staff all my thoughts became hazy. Over the past few years I had experienced various mental difficulties, but nothing like this. I started panicking and went out to the back patio to try and reign in my thoughts. My ability to think felt almost completely broken and incapable of processing information. I gazed up at the trees and sky because I thought it might be the last image I saw before I totally lost my mind. I was afraid I was going to go insane and would have to be taken care of for the rest of my life. As I fought to retain a fraction of mental cohesion I cried out to God in my heart to rescue me. As soon as I reached out to Him my ability to control my thoughts returned. God had brought me back from the edge of insanity. Even though I was in extreme mental distress God showed me he was still in complete control. Once I regained my mental composure I was confident enough to go back inside with the others. Even though the Lord delivered me from that mental distress, my overall strength was still critically low.

I had to dig down each morning to even find the energy to get out of bed. One morning when I awoke and got out of bed, I tried to take my first step and I almost audibly heard my body say, "You can't go any further." My feet suddenly felt encased in lead and all I could do was fall back onto my bed. I had been surviving for so long on sheer will, but now that was even gone. Years before I had determined in my heart I was going to do everything within my power to find happiness and as I lie pinned to my bed, I knew I had. Most importantly, if I was about to die, I was entirely confident I stayed faithful to the Lord until the very end.

I had done all I could on my own, but now I had to reach out for help. I needed professional medical intervention and I knew medication would be part of it. Up until then I didn't want to take any medicine because I thought if God wanted to heal me, he would miraculously do it without any drugs. Even though taking medication didn't 'line up' with my preconceived notion of how I thought God would heal me, I was now willing to take it. I wasn't confident enough in the doctors though to blindly trust whatever treatment they would decide on for me. I needed a health advocate because they would help me discern what was going on and help me decide what to consent to. I believed my mother would be the best choice because she obviously knew me my entire life, as well as that she was a nurse which would enable her to have an objective medical view.

I hadn't told my mother how ill I was so when I called her to ask for help, she was shocked to hear how sick I was. She said of course she would help but it would take her a couple days to drive there. (She lived in New Mexico). I agonized at the thought of having to hang on that much longer and pleaded with God to miraculously keep me alive until she arrived and I started my treatment. I knew there was a possibility I might soon die but I was comforted by the fact that if I did, I would immediately be with my Heavenly Father.

Beginning of healing

As soon as my mother arrived she called my doctor's office to make an appointment; they said to bring me right in. As we drove there I asked her what her initial impression of my health was when she first saw me and she said I looked extremely ill. The way she described how I looked only confirmed how ill I felt. When we arrived they immediately brought me into an examination room. Following are some of the notes from the exam.

6/2/2000

30-year-old male made an appointment today because he said, "he cannot move." He says he feels like a "wet rag." He said, "I don't know if I can take care of myself anymore." In response to the question if he was battling any major issues at the time, he said, "I don't have any issues gnawing in my head" and "I am calm and at peace inside." He says he has been feeling especially weak, more than usual. He sleeps well at night. When suggested he might have depression, he was resistant. He denies any thoughts of harming himself.

Objective Observation:
Overwhelming fatigue, suspect it is a manifestation of depression.

When my doctor described my fatigue as 'overwhelming', he was completely accurate. One meaning of the word 'overwhelming' is defined in the Merriam Webster dictionary as: "To cover over (something) entirely with water". My depression was drowning me, but only I knew how close to dying I was. My doctor was a general practitioner and not a psychiatrist, so he wasn't an expert on assessing how ill I was. He said I needed to see a specialist so he made an emergency appointment with a highly regarded psychiatrist; I felt I was going to finally receive the treatment I desperately needed.

When my mother and I arrived at the psychiatrists office I eagerly awaited my turn. When it was my turn I went right in and began spilling out how I felt. I told him my energy had been draining from me for years and that I knew I soon wouldn't have any left. He said he was amazed I lasted that long without any medical intervention. After sharing for the entire visit, he told me I was suffering from severe clinical depression. I told him I had been diagnosed with that before, but didn't believe it. He explained that depression can progress subtly over years so that is why I probably wasn't aware of it; subsequently, the reason why I resisted the diagnosis. I still didn't fully understand what was happening to me but because I was so sick; I accepted by faith that I had clinical depression. He gave me a prescription and ironically, I couldn't wait to get it filled.

After my mother and I went to the pharmacy and got my medication, we went back to my apartment and I went straight to the bathroom to take my first pill. I opened the bottle and placed one of the small blue pills in my hand. In spite of how extremely ill I was, I unbelievably asked myself, "Should I really take this thing? I don't know what it will do to me; maybe it will make me crazy or fundamentally change my personality!" To fight my fears I trusted the Lord to keep me safe just as I did in the depths of my depression; I needed to apply that same faith to my uncertainties of taking this medication. I hesitantly swallowed the pill and then went to lay down on my bed to await the affects.

Later that day I felt a sensation like small pulses of electricity traveling throughout my body. Over my lifetime my depression had continually robbed me of my energy and now for the first time, I felt it returning. I know people might be highly skeptical of how quickly I felt the affects of my medication, but it is true. The only explanation I can think of was that I was so close to dying that I felt even the most minute improvement. As I lie on my bed I raised my hands and praised God because I knew I was finally receiving the healing I longed for.

Because of my personal experience I now know God uses medicine to perform miracles of healing. God is the one who created our bodies and is also the one who knows how to heal them. He gives wisdom to the people who create these medications that treat our illnesses and ailments.

The brain is the same as all the organs in the sense that it is not immune from illnesses. Since the brain directs the proper functioning of the entire body, when it is damaged the whole body suffers. When someone has a mental illness treatment of it needs to be a priority since the brain is the 'conductor' of the body. Unfortunately, there is still a major societal denial about the reality and seriousness of mental illnesses and how much it destroys people's health and lives.

I needed to go back to New Mexico to live with my mother during the early stages of my recuperation because I wasn't able to care for myself. Before we could leave though I had to wait a few days until I had the strength to travel. Once I felt strong enough I packed some of my things, told my cats I would see them soon and then we started our long trip out. The closer we got to the state line the more anxious I became. I felt that crossing the border was my final step of overcoming my agoraphobia. As soon as I saw the sign 'Leaving New York' panic gripped my heart and I prayed intently for the Lord to keep me calm and safe. Time seemed to slow as we passed under the 'Leaving New York' sign and then under the 'Welcome to Pennsylvania' sign. When we were over the boarder I had a great sense of relief and accomplishment. The further we drove the less I focused on my fears and torment and more on my new life in New Mexico.

Once in New Mexico my whole world was contained in my mother's house and small backyard.

Since my depression had ravaged my mental and physical health for years, all I could do in the beginning was take my medication, rest, sleep, eat and piddle around the house. After about a week on the couch and chair on the back porch; I regained enough strength to walk around and even lightly play fetch with my mother's dog. She had a large butterfly bush in her yard and every day I enjoyed its fragrant little clusters of purple flowers. Depression dulls the senses, so being able to smell the sweetness of those flowers was a pleasant milestone in my recuperation process.

I used to take for granted my ability to think clearly and articulate my thoughts, but not anymore. I now knew what it was like to be on the verge of losing control of my mind, so I was extremely grateful when my ability to concentrate returned. My long and short-term memory were also improving and I was able to remember things I thought I had forgotten forever. I also began seeing the world in a new light and realizing how much my depression distorted my perception of it, especially my understanding of people and my interactions with them. Each day I looked forward to improvements in my health, instead of worrying about if I would survive the day.

After the first couple weeks I began taking short walks on the nearby bike path. I had grown up in an area with plenty of water, trees and grass; but during my walks in New Mexico I mostly saw sand, Juniper trees, Yucca plants and Chamisa bushes. I enjoyed this unfamiliar landscape and the stark contrast it was from the type of landscape I grew up in because even the outdoors didn't remind me of where I had suffered for so long. I felt like being in a completely different environment was a symbol of my new life.

After about a month of recuperation I was mentally and physically strong enough to return to New York to get the rest of my belongings and close out that part of my life. I prayed earnestly for days leading up to my departure because I was consciously going to the one place I never wanted to see again. I had a subconscious fear that the darkness that almost consumed me when I lived there would pull me back in and never let go. Despite my fear and terrible memories, the Lord gave me the strength and courage to go back.

After my flight had arrived in New York, I went directly over to my apartment. When I pulled up in front of the apartment building I looked up at my darkened living room window and immediately started fending off the dreadful memories. While I lived there I daily endured a never-ending barrage of harmful and depressing thoughts, physical suffering and emotional and spiritual torture. I continually fought my dark enemy there as it wrapped tighter around me; squeezing the life out of me. I struggled to survive every minute of every in the dark isolation of that apartment.

As I entered the building and was walking up the stairs I prayed for the Lord to give me the courage to go into my apartment. Once I reached the front door I took a few moments to mentally prepare before I went in. When I was ready, I turned the key and opened the door. I looked around and everything was covered in fine dust and the air was stale. I felt like I was looking at a crime scene because it was where my depression had tortured me for two years. I quickly turned my attention to my cats as they bolted out from behind the couch to greet me. My neighbor fed them when I was gone, but they were still essentially alone the entire time. I immediately knelt down and showered them with affection.

As I walked through the apartment I felt strangely detached because I felt I had lived there in a different lifetime. Everything was in the same place as when I'd left, but I could now clearly see the unkempt conditions I lived in. If someone had visited me while I lived there they would've certainly seen I was having a difficult time caring for myself. I didn't waste any time and quickly began packing. As I got my things together I tried to block out the dark memories of when I lived there.

When I was finished packing I eagerly waited for the movers to arrive. When they got there they packed most of my things and started their trip out to New Mexico. I proceeded to pack the remainder of my belongings in my car and when I was done, I went back in for one last look around to see if I had forgotten anything. After my final walkthrough I quickly headed for the door. When I'd moved out of places I lived in the past I would briefly turn around when I reached the doorway to reflect on some memories of when I lived there. As I left there I didn't turn around for a moment, but rather fixed my eyes firmly ahead. I got in my car, looked in the back seat at my cats in their carriers and drove away from there for the last time.

A new life

When I arrived back in New Mexico I spent a couple more weeks recuperating at my mother's house until I felt strong enough to start venturing out into the world. I was scared because I didn't know what to expect on so many levels. For the first time in years I would be interacting with society without my depression distorting every thought. The first place I wanted to go was church because I wanted to thank God for delivering me from my life of torment. I found a church listed in the phone book that appealed to me so I planned to attend that Sunday.

I was extremely nervous as I entered the church so I slipped into the last pew as inconspicuously as I could. The pastor's message was about new seasons in people's lives and as he preached the Lord told me that my old life of cold and darkness was over and I was in a new season of warmth and light. During my long drive out to New Mexico I hoped I would feel the Lord's presence as much there as I had back in New York. As God spoke to me during the message, I knew he was with me as much here as he was two thousand miles away. The Lord kept me alive and sane in the darkness and I was now certain he would be as close to me in my new life.

The more time I spent exploring the area where I now lived, the more comfortable I felt being outside my mother's house. After a few weeks of acclimating to my new surroundings I felt ready to find my own place to live. A couple days after I started my search God led me to the exact apartment I was looking for. On the first day in my new home I lay down on the carpet in my empty living room and let out a huge sigh of relief. I felt a tremendous amount of stress flow down through me and into the carpet. After years of moving around and battling my depression, I could finally rest.

Now that I had my own apartment the next step in my new life was to find a job. When I was very sick I'd squeaked out an existence by taking whatever work I could find but that wouldn't suffice this time. I now lived in a tourist destination so the cost of living was higher. I knew I had to find a job that paid much more than one standing behind a cash register. I wanted to teach in some capacity because it was what I was good at and what I went to school for. To have an impressive resume though I knew I had to have a substantial amount of teaching experience. Because of my deficient work history it was impossible to massage my resume enough to make it appear I was a good candidate for a teaching position. Being a substitute teacher and having a string of minimum wage jobs would definitely not impress a desired employer. I knew I was not going to get hired based on my experience so I had to trust the Lord to miraculously supply me one. I had faith that whatever job He provided, it would pay enough to enable me to support myself. Since I had just been to the edge of death and back, I felt trusting the Lord to find me the type of job I needed was an easy stroll through the park of faith.

After about two weeks of searching for work I was talking with a gentleman in church and told him I was looking for a job. He said he was a supervisor at (one of the state agencies in New Mexico) and he needed to hire a trainer for his office. He started describing what the job entailed and the more he did, the more excited I became because it was the exact type of position I was looking for. He said he was conducting interviews that Wednesday and asked if I was interested in coming in and I said I definitely was. My interview went well and he then offered me the position; it paid more than three times as much as the highest paying job I'd ever had. Even though I knew God promised he would provide for me I was still amazed when he answered my prayer so perfectly and timely!

At my new job I taught a wide variety of subjects such as Making Meetings Work, Stress Management, Presentation Skills, First Aid/CPR, Defensive Driving, Computer Skills and a variety of others. Sometimes when I was up in front of a class teaching I thought how amazing God is because he took me from barely being able to have a lucid thought to teaching employees how to increase their professional work skills. Even though I was able to teach, I was still very much in the early stages of my healing. I struggled to have enough mental and physical energy to make it through each day but fortunately I was blessed with a lot of 'down time' at this job. I had to take my medication throughout the day and sometimes I needed to when I was teaching. I didn't want my students to see me take me pills so I devised some sly techniques so they wouldn't. I didn't want other employees to know I had clinical depression because there is often a prejudice in the workplace that a person with a mental illness cannot perform their job as well, or better, than employees without one. If someone with a mental illness is healthy they are just as capable to succeed as anyone else.

I had a major scare during the early stages of my recovery because my depression reemerged. When I felt the symptoms return I didn't hesitate to seek medical attention. To receive the best care I prayed for wisdom and guidance to choose the right psychiatrist. The first two I tried didn't counsel me much, they just had me try a few different medications. It was very scary having to wait and see how each one interacted with my brain chemistry; all I could do was trust the Lord that he was in control during this trial-and-error process. None of the medications worked and I think they genuinely didn't care. I felt like I was just one of the cattle they herded through their offices so they could collect their exorbitant fees afterwards.

The third psychiatrist I went to was much more attentive and genuinely concerned about my recovery. During my initial visit he gave me an extensive questionnaire to help him evaluate my mental condition and after he studied the results he reaffirmed my original diagnoses of clinical depression. Since I had already taken multiple medications without any results he said there were two more we could try and if they didn't work, he didn't know of any others that might. The first medication he prescribed didn't work and then there was just the one left. I was scared that if this last one didn't work I could permanently live in a dark and solitary world. After taking the new medication for a few days I started experiencing sustained improvement. I praised God for guiding me safely through the maze of doctors and medications to arrive at a successful treatment.

I didn't just take my medication and automatically get better though; I was proactive in the process. The major physical components of my recovery were taking my medication, eating right, occasional exercise and getting a lot of physical and mental rest. Because I had to rest a lot, I am sure people around me thought I was lazy because I didn't do much outside of my house. I often felt the pressure to get out and do more but because I knew I needed to rest, I refrained. I did everything I could to expedite my recovery because I didn't want anything to delay it in any way. It wasn't easy and I often feared my depression would return but I looked to the Lord for the faith and courage to continue on.

When my depression was the worst I could barely get off the floor or think straight. I have now regained enough strength that at my new job I was able to pick-axe through shale-like clay for a week. I now have the mental endurance and clarity of mind that enabled me to write this book. When I wake in the morning I am no longer afraid if I will survive the day; rather I think of what I need to do and am able to accomplish it. Now that I have regained my physical and mental strength I am determined not to forget all the Lord taught me during my years in the darkness. I try to continue to reach out to Him with all my heart as earnestly as I did when I was clinging to my life and sanity.

I have found a godly church that I have been attending for five years. I meet weekly with a group from my church and we support and encourage one another personally and in our faith. When I am in the midst of enjoying our fellowship my heart rejoices because I am no longer trapped in my solitary world of torment. When we share our personal struggles the group is quick to support each other. I grew to trust them enough that one week I took a step of faith and opened up about the years of my torturous depression; prior to then I was afraid if I did they would've stereotyped me and viewed me as 'not as godly' as them. As I shared they attentively listened and weren't judgmental and it felt wonderful. Once I shared I let go of my fear of being rejected because of what I went through. Strangely enough, in a way it was more difficult to tell others my story face-to-face than sharing it with the world in this book.

It is now 2017 and I am forty-eight. It took me about eighteen years to descend into the deepest parts of my depression and about the same amount of time to climb out to where I am today. When I was in counseling I told my counselor that I always had a desire to help others who were hurting inside. He told me that before I could help anyone else I first needed to be whole myself. I praise God because now that He healed me I can fulfill the desire of my heart and help others by sharing my story of triumph over depression.

Printed in Great
Britain
by Amazon